THE
BLUEPRINT

HOW TO DESIGN AND LIVE A LIFE
OF AUTHENTICITY AND PURPOSE

TRELLIS USHER

THE BLUEPRINT:
How To Design and Live A Life of Authenticity and Purpose
Copyright © 2018, T.R. Ellis Group LLC

Printed in the United States of America

First Printing, 2018

ISBN (Print Edition): 978-1-54392-180-9
ISBN (eBook Edition): 978-1-54392-181-6

Credits
Cover Design – Joshua Jadon
Back cover photo – Darnell Wilburn
T.R. Ellis Group LLC

Publishing Division
Atlanta, Georgia USA

T.R. ELLIS GROUP

Dedication

For always believing in and fighting for me until I developed the courage to do it for myself. I miss your physical presence, but you are never far from my heart. I love you mom. This one's for you!

TABLE OF CONTENTS

THE BIRTH OF THE
BLUEPRINT FRAMEWORK

"It takes courage to grow up and become who you really are."

– E. E. CUMMINGS

We came together to smile and laugh. We drank great wine and enjoyed delicious food. We discussed our careers and we shared our deepest hopes and dreams for the future. We gave advice and we told stories. There was laughter and tears (and sometimes both at the same time).

Whenever one of these gatherings of friends takes place, someone, whether they like it or not, inevitably steps forward as the designated coach.

I'm a corporate consultant focused on helping to transform organizations and their leaders, and that means whenever my friends and I get together like this, I'm usually the one they turn to for coaching and advice. I often deal with behavior models and frameworks as part of the consulting I deliver in my day job, and, as the years have gone by, I've often found myself applying similar models and frameworks to the personal transformation conversations I have with my friends and members of my family.

In fact, several years ago, the stories and antidotes we shared began to morph into a vision for an entire self-improvement and life coaching framework. I started to wonder what kind of impact I could make if the framework that was taking shape wasn't limited to just my group of close friends. I started imagining what could happen if I took my years of experience and expertise helping Fortune 100 companies develop the best leaders and teams along with the insights that were taking shape in my mind and create a program for personal transformation? I've spent nearly two decades being trained by some of the best companies in the world in what it takes to transform leaders and organizations and much of that formal classroom and on-the-job training is applicable for personal transformation as well.

It was from these humble beginnings that the personal transformation framework you now hold in your hands was formulated.

In 2011, I began running live workshops and retreats where I led participants through *The Blueprint* process I'd developed and tested with my friends over the years. I loved watching people apply the framework to their lives, and I was particularly thrilled when workshop participants began experiencing life-changing results. With now proven results from *The Blueprint* in hand, I felt ready to conquer anything life could throw my way.

But in 2014, everything changed.

After my annual exam and subsequent visits to a breast specialist and radiologist, I was informed that I had developed Triple Negative Breast Cancer (TNBC).

Much of the stability I'd taken for granted was thrown askew. I saw my life from angles I'd never considered before. Everything from my emotional wellbeing, to my spirituality, to my family's financial status was immediately more relevant and pressing than just the day before. I was blessed and fortunate that my diagnosis wasn't terminal. The breast cancer wasn't metastatic, but the diagnosis none-the-less lit a fire beneath me.

The Blueprint was something I'd been developing for years, and I had led clients and workshop attendees through it with great success. But the cancer brought with it a startling realization: I'd been using *The Blueprint* on a purely intellectual level. Building a dream life had been a theoretical exercise. It was only once I began my battle with breast cancer that I internalized the process for the first time and started applying *The Blueprint* to my life on every level

– not just the intellectual. Health, wellness, and my soul's purpose became the lens through which I evaluated my life's status and direction.

I was fighting for my life and the security of my children, and when those are the stakes it becomes a lot easier to make difficult but necessary decisions about where your life is headed. I wasn't interested in carrying with me anything that wasn't going to be useful on my journey towards health. My life became the ultimate research lab for the system I'd developed.

Happily, *The Blueprint* proved to be an extraordinary tool for rebuilding a life on every level. The advice I'd been giving for years became real and tangible in a way it never had before. I approached my own *Blueprint* work in a holistic manner and I saw amazing results during one of the most difficult times in my life.

I urge you to keep this in mind as you apply the material to *your* life. You can approach *The Blueprint* from a purely intellectual level and think about it in terms of setting goals and creating to-do lists for different areas of your life. It will certainly be effective if you approach it in this way, but it can be *so much more powerful than that*. Approaching your life renovation project holistically means including the intellectual, emotional, and spiritual aspects of who you are. It will allow you to achieve a well-rounded life that's fulfilling on all levels. It has changed my life, the lives of many of my clients, and I know it can change yours as well.

Introduction:
This is **YOUR** Life

"If I didn't define myself for myself, I would be crunched into other people's fantasies for me and eaten alive."

— AUDRE LORDE

This book is for people who have hit a bump in the road and are facing challenges in their lives. It could be a sobering health condition like my cancer diagnosis; it may be a threat to your financial stability, like losing your job; it might even be relationship-based, like losing a loved one or the dissolving of a marriage. These types of events have a tremendous impact on our lives and will often drive us to seek out deeper purpose and meaning. That said, you don't have to be facing a great catastrophe to benefit from what this book has to offer.

Many people have an inner knowing that their lives could have more of an impact on the world that they have so far. They want to discover how to change their lives for the better. They sense incongruity or lack of authenticity about the way they've been going about their lives, and they want to explore and address it. Of course, many people are still in survival mode, just trying to meet the challenges of everyday life, but increasing numbers of people are waking up to the possibility of something more.

Perhaps you feel you're a mixture of these groups, or maybe something else entirely brought you to this book. Whatever the reason, rest assured: if you're passionate about making changes by putting into action what you learn within these pages, you'll make significant progress towards achieving your dreams.

A Life that Fits

Leaving a 16-year corporate career behind to start my own company seemed like an odd choice to many who knew me. I was fortunate to have found my passion early. When I stepped into my first role as a corporate trainer, I felt at home. I was helping people perform their jobs better. I was helping them feel better about their work and thereby improving the overall organization.

Despite having a few things working against me, I worked hard to succeed. I was recently divorced, now a young single mother and rather than completing college immediately after high school, I ran off to Hawaii and married my high school sweetheart. I loved the work I was doing as a corporate trainer. It mattered to me. So, 16 years later when I told close friends and family that I was leaving a cushy executive job with a globally recognized brand to start my own business, I got a few confused looks.

It's not easy to live a life that "fits". A life that fits who you are but can also expand to fit who you are becoming. A life filled with extraordinary joy, kindness, and serenity is the result of taking actions that expose you to the attention of others. Some of the attention will come as the well-deserved result of hard work and dedication. Unfortunately, putting yourself out there will also attract the attention of naysayers and haters. People may criticize and ostracize you, or they may try to convince you the way you've chosen to live your life is a mistake. In response to these sorts of attacks, you may feel compelled to abandon your journey towards authenticity and simply blend in.

We must intentionally and persistently strive to be the people we know we're capable of being, especially in the face of adversity and disbelief. That's why I'm excited you have the courage and determination to invest your time and energy in designing, building, and living an extraordinary dream life – a life that fits and one that matters to you.

Too many of us go about our lives making decisions based on the needs, perceptions, expectations, and limits imposed by others. Often our entire way of being is based on other people's opinions, rather than who our hearts tell us we can become. We compromise because we believe the people giving us advice or picking apart our decisions have our best interests at heart – and often they do. Some of the people who knowingly or inadvertently place limits on us include our closest friends, family members, mentors, and loved ones. We are conditioned to heed their advice along with all of the cultural, gender, racial, religious, and geographic norms that we are born into, but it's time to realize no one is more invested in your life than *you* are. Your life is like your home – you can't expect your neighbors or your family members to come over and repave the driveway, repair the roof or add on a new room for you; you must do the work yourself.

Your Life as a House

If you were to compare the current state of your life to a house, there's a good chance you might describe it as old, run down, dilapidated... maybe even falling apart. And if I was to ask you how your life feels right now, you might use words like cramped, outdated, poorly maintained, boring or cluttered. You aren't alone. Most people's lives can use some major renovation. Day after day, we ignore opportunities for improvement. Most of us wait until we're forced into action before making changes of any kind. In addition, many of us have negative self-perceptions that don't accurately represent the true state of our lives.

We all have areas in need of improvement, but we also have areas in which we excel. Each of us has natural talents and access to existing resources. These are the key building blocks of who you are and who you can become. Recognizing these traits and learning to value and cherish them is an important part of your overall self-improvement project.

———————————————————————————

I strongly believe that tapping into purpose is the fastest and most sustainable driver for success. Not simply the trappings of success but true internal, emotional and spiritual success.

———————————————————————————

You have an incredible opportunity ahead of you because you're about to become a visionary architect with the power and ability to design the life of your dreams. You'll also be the general contractor and builder responsible for taking the actions necessary to achieve the completed dream home. Best of all, you get to be the client, which means once you're done building the home of your dreams, you're the one who gets to enjoy the fruits of your labor by living within what you have constructed.

If you could design a home that fits who you are right now, but could also expand to include who you're becoming – your future goals and dreams – what would that home look like? How would it make you feel about yourself and your life? This book is going to help you answer these questions. *The Blueprint* will guide you through the process of creating a life that makes you feel fulfilled. Fulfilled because this work will bring you into alignment with your God-given, Universal purpose. I strongly believe that tapping into purpose is the fastest and most sustainable driver for success. Not simply the trappings of success but true internal, emotional and spiritual success. You won't ignore your current responsibilities or the expectations of those important to you, but the process is going to first focus on *your* needs, *your* expectations, and *your* dreams. This journey is not about shaping your life to the desires of your friends, family, or coworkers; it's about achieving what you want to achieve.

Each of us is born possessing all we need within us to do incredible things and that includes *you*. Life, with all of its twists and turns and ups and downs, is a grand journey. If we approach that journey with a growth-focused, optimistic, and accepting mindset, we're able to discover the truth about what we can achieve.

Through inquiry, introspection, discussion, and a little bit of good ol' fashioned elbow grease, this book will help you:

- Recognize self-limiting beliefs that might be keeping you from living your dreams,

- Clarify your personal vision statement and comprehensive life plan,

- Recognize and address fears, distractions and barriers that are keeping you from reaching your goals,

- question and uncover the real motivations behind your intentions and fears

Throughout each chapter, you'll find descriptions of the different metaphorical "rooms" of your dream house, along with questions to ask yourself about the room's current condition and how you might be able to redesign it so that it feels more aligned with who you are becoming on your journey of transformation. Room by room, you'll need to define what your dream life is going to look, sound, and feel like. This vision will hold your intentions for your new life, and will help keep you accountable when distractions and challenges arise (as they inevitably will).

It's only when knowledge is applied, reinforced and repeated that it becomes embedded as a regular practice. As such, this book includes several exercises designed to walk you through essential elements in *The Blueprint* framework and then put them into practice. Be sure to complete each exercise as you work your way through the book. They will form the basis of your personal blueprint.

Some of the exercises may make you feel uncomfortable. That's *good*. Each exercise, if approached with mindfulness and intention, will contribute to shaking up your life, at least a little bit, and will move you closer to living a life of authenticity and purpose.

1

DISCOVERING WHAT
MATTERS MOST

"Defining myself, as opposed to being defined by others,
is one of the most difficult challenges I face."

– CAROL MOSELEY-BRAUN

I often refer to myself as a "spiritual mutt" because throughout my life, I've spent time studying and fellowshipping with people of different religious beliefs. I wasn't aware at the time but those intimate conversations either one on one or with a small group were refining, or in some cases reshaping my beliefs and values altogether. I was beginning to understand more clearly that the "letter and spirit" of spiritual laws are both necessary but distinct in their application to real life. Born into westernized Christianity, southeast United States (The Bible Belt) more specifically, meant that I was handed a set of beliefs that everyone else around me also inherited and any deviation was considered humanistic, blasphemous, and sinful. As I began to mature spiritually and learn more about the world and others in it, many of my long-held beliefs began to shift. Spiritually, I began to resonate with ideals like inclusion, understanding, and listening instead of exclusion, intolerance, and discourse. After getting through the initial misunderstandings, on both sides, with close friends and family members, I am now able to subscribe to spiritual rituals and practices that are authentic for me while standing on the principles and faith of my Christian upbringing. Being willing to acknowledge a sense of dissonance was a hugely important part of my journey and asking questions of myself and my Faith allowed me to gain a sense of clarity concerning my purpose.

The design portion of *The Blueprint* involves clarifying the vision you have for your new life. As with building a physical home, you're going to develop a mental picture, or, as we are going to call in the context of this book, a "Blueprint" of what you want your dream life to look like.

A common challenge people face at this stage is a lack of clarity regarding what they want to achieve, which inevitably leads to a lack of focus going forward. It's easy to get distracted if you don't have a definite destination in mind. As the Cheshire Cat explains to young Alice in Lewis Carroll's *Alice in Wonderland*, if you don't know where you are going, any road will get you there. This work isn't about filling your metaphorical house with every luxury design element you've ever seen. It's about being very intentional about what is needed in your house that will help you in your journey of becoming.

Your Blueprint will help you stay motivated when you feel like giving up. Holding that vision of your life in your mind, heart, and spirit will keep you going through the rain, snow, and cold. (Remember, no one said this was going to be easy!) A clear vision of where you are headed will remind you of the joy and peace you're working towards. It'll also allow you to celebrate the small victories every time you make concrete steps towards achieving what you've set out to accomplish.

Your Blueprint will not be set in stone, so don't feel pressured to make it perfect right away. An architect's key tool isn't her pencil, it's her eraser. When designing a building, she'll regularly use her eraser to refine or even reimagine what the final structure will look like and how it will function. She'll move a wall here, or change a room there, until everything finally fits just as it should. Trying out different design concepts and ideas is all part of the process. Our lives should be based on a clear vision rooted in authenticity. While the vision serves as the anchor, the tactics should be flexible enough for us to pivot when life throws a curve ball our way or when new information and resources come into focus.

I'm a big fan of renovation project television shows and what I've learned from them is renovations never go according to plan. The unexpected twists and turns the projects take are a major source of drama and excitement, and it's the same with our lives. Never quite knowing how things are going to turn out is part of what makes life fun. As the saying goes, "When you make plans, God laughs."

The key to a successful personal transformation is learning to tune in to your inner voice and discover what is authentic for you.

That doesn't mean planning isn't an essential part of executing any successful project. What it means is the best plans, just like the most successful architects, are adaptable. Keep that big architect's eraser in your pocket and be ready to adjust your plans on the fly. As the years go by, you may discover certain skills or tools aren't needed or utilized in the same way they once were; that's completely normal. Your life will look one way when you're a single person, and an entirely different way when you're married, or starting a family. As you grow and change, you'll need to update your blueprint to meet those new needs.

While the blueprint for your dream life is a plan, it's not a static one because life itself isn't static. Your plan changes to fit where you are in your life, as well as where you're going. It expands and contracts according to what your inner voice tells you is right for you.

LISTENING TO YOUR INNER VOICE

Almost from the moment we are born, we are given a set of "conditions" and norms that will govern our entire lives. We are handed an identity based on race, gender, the part of the world we are born into, language, a set of religious traditions, social, political and economic norms. And if that wasn't enough, most people around us for the first couple of decades are given pretty much those same conditions. Those norms are reinforced all around us. It's nearly impossible to discover our uniqueness in an ocean of conformity; to distinguish our inner voice from the cacophony of voices swirling around in our minds.

Your voice matters most at the outset of your journey. The process you're undertaking is personal and unique to you. People in your life will want to give you advice and share their experiences with you when they hear you're embarking on a journey of transformation. It's important to be open to the advice of others, especially those you love, trust, and respect; however, the starting point in this "renovation project" is not the time to prioritize the guidance of others before your own intuition. Be respectful, yet firm, and always remain focused on your vision for your life. No one knows your life's purpose better than you do.

It's likely you got where you are now as the result of heeding the guidance of a myriad of voices that set up shop in your head. Parents, teachers, friends, and colleagues all impose their opinions or worldviews on us throughout our lives. Their voices fill our minds with stories, beliefs, and advice. Despite their best intentions, these voices are the cause of many of the limiting beliefs that hold us back and keep us living small, inauthentic lives. They're the voices saying you aren't good enough, you aren't capable enough, you aren't worthy, and what you want to achieve can never be done. In essence, "who does she think she is?" When most people hear that we feel compelled or "called" to change, they interpret it through their own lens of conformity to mean that "something is wrong with *their* lives" since their lives are likely like ours.

You'll need to summon the courage to confront those voices and evict them from your mind. The only sound you want in your head at this point is your authentic voice – the voice of your inner spirit urging you toward your life's purpose. Your number one goal during the visioning process is to become crystal clear about what your inner voice is telling you.

This clarity won't come quickly. It isn't after a single prayer or one month of quiet reflection and meditation that you'll suddenly understand the truth of what you're meant to do on this Earth. Just as identifying your dream house will be an ongoing process of discovery, so too will be the deepening trust in the inner guidance you receive about what's right for you

As you continue to work through the process, you'll become increasingly confident in your unique talents and gifts. Your inner voice will gradually become the most important voice you heed. When you rely on the agendas, opinions, and advice of others, you can spend years bouncing back and forth between different people's plans and visions for your life. To achieve the goals most important to you, however, it's essential you learn to develop and trust an internal compass that'll direct you toward your real objectives, core beliefs, and true purpose.

**The Rooms of Your House:
The Foundation**

The foundation is unique to each architect because it's made from the core values and beliefs everything else rests upon. It represents what you consider the most important building blocks for your life.

For some people the foundation will be based on finances. These are the people who don't feel stable unless the family is financially secure.

For other people, the foundation may be focused around spirituality, or relationships, or even personal growth and well-being.

The foundation is personal and flexible depending on who you are.

Listen to your inner voice. What is it telling you is most important to you?

LAYING THE FOUNDATION: YOUR CORE BELIEFS

We build our lives on a set of core thoughts, beliefs, and assumptions that together weave an ever-encompassing and seemingly absolute narrative or story. This tapestry serves as the "foundational elements" of your dream life.

Most of us want to create a brand new, authentic and evolving life, but we attempt to build it on a fixed, narrow and shallow set of beliefs that can't accommodate the depth and reach of our dreams.

Tearing up the foundation of your current life is intimidating work. It requires specialized equipment and a lot of determination. It means getting dirty, something we aren't always willing to do. That's why people often try to avoid this step. They think, "No one is ever going to see the foundation, so why put much effort into reinforcing it? A foundation is just a big block of concrete after all."

Indeed, there may not be anything fancy about laying a new foundation and few people will ever see it, much less appreciate it, but any homebuilder will tell you the bigger and grander the structure, the broader and deeper the foundation needs to be to support it.

There's a good chance you've already started chipping away at the outdated and limiting foundations of your current circumstances. You're searching and striving for more purpose in your life. You've probably already developed awareness that you've outgrown your old life. Your soul is crying for more space to stretch out and grow, and that's fantastic. Or maybe your life is screaming that it's too expansive and scattered and you'd benefit from a more focused and minimalistic existence. Embrace those feelings! Just make sure you start your growth by addressing your foundational beliefs.

It's time to decide what beliefs, values, and worldviews from your current life you're going to keep, and which ones you are going to discard.

HOLDING ON AND LETTING GO

You may feel a desire to throw everything away and start from scratch, especially if you're disappointed with your current life. There are, however, things from your current life that'll still be useful in your new life, so don't be too quick toss everything.

Of course, you won't want to keep everything either. If you give in to those hoarding tendencies that make throwing things out so difficult, you'll just have the same life you have now. Everything may look shiny and new in the beginning, but after time you'll realize you've spent a lot of energy, focus, and resources only to reconstruct the same life you already had.

Along with some prompting from the universe, you've decided your life needs to change, but what that change will look like is unique to you. Whether it's a redesign, a renovation, or totally new construction: you'll need to decide what approach is best for you.

As it happens, you'll see that creating a blueprint for the life you want also brings clarity about what you *don't* want. The truth isn't always pleasant, but a lot of life isn't pleasant. That's why we have garbage pick-up. Every week the garbage man stops by the end of your driveway. That's your opportunity to rid yourself of all the things that have served their purpose in your life and have now become waste.

Imagine you never got rid of any of your clothing and instead just kept adding more clothes to your closet. Eventually, the closet would become so full of clutter that you'd never be able to find anything new to wear. The same thing happens to our bodies and our lives when we let things that should be eliminated pile up. You must master the art of letting go of the elements in your life that have outlived their usefulness.

Many of us hold on to habits, beliefs, and people long after they've served their purpose. Some of the furniture in your current house won't be useful in your new dream home. Sometimes the items, ideas, and people that served pivotal roles in your past can be harmful to you if you place them in positions of prominence in your new life.

As you can imagine, being born and raised in the southeastern United States, going to church each week was a big part of my family's life. There was church on Sunday. Bible Study on Wednesday and some youth service on Friday nights. Unlike today, every church had a van or bus that came around and picked up the neighborhood children to make sure we were in church even if our parents were not. Children's Church was the community's way of making sure that we learned the basic tenets of our faith like the Ten Commandments and what was right and wrong in the eyes of God. We were given Bibles and were taught that it was the literal and unwavering Word of God and we were never to question or doubt any of it especially the New Testament words that were in red. It was as if Jesus pierced his actual finger and wrote his own blood those words in every single printed Bible.

One of the messages that was all around me as a young person growing up wanting to please God and Jesus was that homosexuality was a sin and homosexuals were unrepentant sinners. Not the regular sinners like all the rest of us but a different and worse kind. Gay jokes were plentiful and we all laughed at those jokes as young people coming of age in the 80's. But there are people I know who are adults now and they are still laughing and spewing hateful and hurtful words. It wasn't funny then and it certainly isn't funny now.

As I've grown and matured in my own understanding of the love and grace of God, I've had to repent of my past sins of bigotry. While discrimination and harassment have never intentionally or consciously been part of my core values, too often I let others get away with it to fit it or more accurately, not stand out. Once I started my corporate career in Human Resources, I was required to steward the equality and fairness of everyone in the workplace. I got to know many gay people in the LGBTQI community and began to question many of the beliefs I'd been taught by the larger society and held for most of my teenage and young adult life. Working amongst diverse individuals throughout my career has taught me three important life lessons. First, if you define a person's life based on one aspect of it, you're going to always be wrong about who they really are. Second, you're also likely to see yourself through a cracked lens which is detrimental to your own emotional and spiritual growth. And finally, no matter our sexual orientation, all of us basically want to be loved, valued, heard and accepted. For me to move into my purpose, I had to acknowledge that beliefs I'd held as absolute truths were essentially nothing more than a bunch of unreliable assumptions. Once I came to grips with this, I had to have the courage to let them go. Far too often, my clients, friends, and family members express their feelings of sheer exhaustion. They say their lives have become so very *heavy*. They're constantly battling burnout, and weighed down by the burdens of carrying around beliefs and habits that are no longer of use to them.

You know those boxes you tucked away in the attic (or stacked in the corner of your basement) that have been sitting there for years, still unpacked? We transfer the unopened boxes from house to house without ever deciding what to do with their contents. Those same sorts of figurative boxes exist in our lives in the form of outdated beliefs and relationships. There's no denying we get nostalgic pleasure from taking the occasional trip down memory lane, but if you still have boxes of parachute pants, cassettes tapes, and every elementary school art project your kids ever completed stored away, it's probably time to do some unpacking and purging.

In her book *The Life-Changing Magic of Tidying Up*, Marie Kondo recommends the following process for deciding what to keep and what needs to be thrown away: "Take each item in one's hand and ask: "Does this spark joy?" If it does, keep it. If not, dispose of it. This is not only the simplest but also the most accurate yardstick by which to judge."

It's time to let go of the things that don't bring you joy and are potential sources of pain for others.

#SizeMatters

Creating a dream home doesn't always mean a more lavish and spacious environment than where you currently rest your head. In fact, after your initial visioning exercise, you might decide to *downsize* your life. Perhaps you'll find you actually prefer a minimalist and streamlined lifestyle. I've seen clients envision and create their blueprint from this perspective, especially when they realize many of the things they've collected over the years have become stress-inducing or limiting their freedom in some manner.

I often think about the sense of peace I felt when I walked into a new model home that's staged with only the necessary functional furnishings and a select few decorative pieces. The pale colored or neutral walls immediately helped me to feel calm and relaxed. Some people like their lives to feel that way: calm, serene, and minimalist. Of course, others value vibrantly colored walls, and the furnishings, pictures, and books to compliment. Some people prefer lots of open space for entertaining, while others prefer their homes to be intimate and cozy. Both approaches are fine. It's about what works best for you and your life that matters.

Leadership and Life Coach and a good friend of mine Kevin A. Johnson, always asks his coaching clients, "What makes you come alive?" It's a great question because those sources of "aliveness" need to be part of your foundation. What you're after is alignment between your lifestyle and your life's purpose. By doing this work, you'll gain authenticity and congruency between what's inside and what's outside. It all starts with letting go of what doesn't work, so you can make room for what does.

Size matters, but bigger isn't always better. For some people less is better, and for others more is what they need. Don't get caught in the trap of comparing the size of your life to someone else's life. It's about identifying, and then leaning into, what is true for you.

We become so attached to how we've always thought about things that we almost never stop to ask ourselves, "Is this *still* true for me?" Asking the question doesn't automatically mean you should discard the thoughts, values, beliefs, and traditions you've grown-up with. It may turn out, after you've unpacked and evaluated them, you're more certain than ever they're right and true for you. But an unwillingness to ask the questions in the first place can result in unstable and unreliable faith in the values you hold dear. If it's never been tested, how can you place your absolute trust in it? How do you know it really matters if you're too afraid to explore it?

You may also discover you've packed away something you now need but didn't value at the time you put it away. wOr, perhaps in haste – due to anger, pain, rejection, or simply in an attempt to avoid unpleasant emotions – you tossed aside valuable belongings without asking yourself if you were going to need them later on. In the same way that there are belongings you've kept that you should've discarded, there are also things you've discarded that you'll wish you'd held onto.

As we mature, and come face-to-face with the responsibilities of life, we often lose the joy, playfulness, and vulnerability of our youth. We devalue core pieces of ourselves because we were hurt or betrayed. Someone told us that we were "too much of this" or "not enough of that" and we believed them, so we packed up our heart's desires and tucked away parts of ourselves in the basement. Fast-forward five, ten, or fifteen years, and it feels like something is missing—has this happened to you? You remember it, finally, but can't recall the last time you saw it or where you put it. You search for the missing piece in other people, in status and achievements, or maybe in the thrill of a life of excess, but all to no avail. It—that quality, that dream, vision, or big life goal—still feels lost to you. My hope is that through this journey of renovating or rebuilding your life, you'll rediscover some of those beautiful and useful things you packed away long ago. I hope you'll put them out on display in your new life in a place of prominence where they belong.

EXERCISE: YOUR HIGHEST SELF

Take a few minutes to reflect on what you perceive to be the best and highest version of yourself. With your eyes closed, sit in silence for five or six minutes, and envision that person carefully. Pay attention to how you feel while you're thinking about that person and that life – your life.

After you've spent time reflecting, open your eyes and answer these two questions:

"At my best, who am I?"

"Who am I becoming?"

Now write down your answers.

This exercise is dynamic. Later, you may think about something that didn't occur to you immediately, and you'll go back and add it to the page. You won't think of everything on this first pass, but you'll have opened a gate for new thoughts to begin to flow into your consciousness.

You'll continue to receive inspiration in the days to come. Let that knowledge flow freely into your conscious mind. Resist the temptation to resist or judge it.

Your Highest Self

Who am I?

_____

_____

_____

_____

Who Am I becoming?

_____

_____

_____

_____

2

START WITH GRATITUDE

"Let gratitude be the pillow upon which you kneel to say your nightly prayer. And let faith be the bridge you build to overcome evil and welcome good."

— MAYA ANGELOU

I say quite often that the breast cancer community is the best community that I never wanted to be a part of. By that I mean that while I would have never wished for a breast cancer diagnosis, now having come through it I wouldn't trade the experience for anything. I'm grateful for my cancer diagnosis. I'm grateful for every chemo infusion. Every surgery. Every dose of radiation and even for the few scars still left on my slightly asymmetrical breast. But mostly I'm grateful for every person in my tribe who went through the journey with me. I'm grateful for every person on my healthcare team at Northside Hospital Cancer Care Center. I'm grateful for my breast surgeon and my plastic surgeon. I'm grateful for the other patients and survivors that have encouraged me. I'm grateful for the team at Ford Automotive for their Models of Courage and Warriors in Pink campaign that provides me with a vehicle to give back to a community that has given and continues to give so much to me. The list goes on and on and on, but the underlying sentiment is gratitude.

There are four cornerstones that define my life and my life's purpose. They are God, Grace, Generosity and Gratitude. My 4G's.

The decision to act and make big changes in your life can be overwhelming.

When thinking about the "good life" too many people envision wealth, fame, and beauty. They focus on external changes like flat stomachs, walk-in closets full of shoes, and a slew of other things they've been told symbolize success, health, and happiness. Before they've even started their journey, they're already mentally projecting into a future they've all been told is right for them.

The Rooms of Your House: The Study

The study addresses the need for life-long learning. It includes formal, informal, collaborative, and emotional learning. The Study is a place of reading and research. It's a quiet place where you can also think and reflect.

The key questions to ask yourself here are:

- Am I open to learning and trying new things?
- Am I continuing to improve and develop my knowledge?
- What new skills am I working to develop right now?

When we project into the future in this manner, we lose sight of what's right in front of us. Achieving success in the future can't come at the expense of the many wonderful blessings in the form of joy, peace, accomplishments, relationships, and possessions we already have right now. By embracing what we currently have with gratitude and acceptance, we make our first major steps towards achieving our future goals.

As your first step towards changing your life, I recommend something much easier than trying to project yourself into a future life without an understanding of how you're going to get there or what advantages you're already starting with. Instead, I invite you to stop for a moment, take a deep breath, and then honestly acknowledge the current state of your life. Take a few seconds to forget the past, ignore the future, and focus your attention on this moment. Exist in the present, breathe it in, and then speak three words to the Universe: "Yes," and "Thank you."

The "Yes" confirms your acceptance of your current reality, and the "Thank you" expresses your gratitude for it.

Slowing down to be present with the current moment is something most of us do rarely, if ever. But before you can focus on where you eventually want to get to, or who you want to become, you must first come to terms with who you are and where you are in your life. By "coming to terms with who you are and where you are", I don't mean just acknowledging it; rather, I mean accepting it. I mean letting go of the resentment, anger, hurt, and disappointment at all the times life didn't turn out the way you expected it would. None of us has a crystal ball to see into the future, and we all make mistakes along the way. Where we end up in life can be completely out of our control. We can't change the past and no one knows what the future will bring. All we can do is accept the current state of our "house", i.e. our current station in life, as our starting point.

Your life may not be perfect (it's probably not), it may not be what you dreamed it would be when you were young (it almost certainly isn't), but it's yours, and it *is* the perfect place to begin your journey.

Some people's starting point may be further along than yours, but there are also people way behind you. Each of our personal journeys takes its own path. Even in cases where your life experiences seem like someone else, you'll eventually discover your desires, fears, and passions are distinctly your own. That's what makes you unique. Taking the time to appreciate who you are, where you are, and how you got here is necessary before you embark on the next leg in your journey.

I don't want you to begrudgingly acknowledge where you are in your life. I don't want you to resent your life or feel ashamed by your current personal or professional status. Instead, I urge you to embrace the complication and find beauty in it. Be grateful for who you are because you're full of beauty and infinite potential.

The most successful people I know practice consistent, abiding gratitude. That doesn't mean they want to remain where they are forever. Instead, it demonstrates an understanding that sustainable progress cannot be achieved from a place of self-loathing and disgust. Success in any area of life starts from a position of gratitude. It's deeper than simply an "attitude of gratitude" that you can put on or take off like an overcoat; it's actually *being* grateful. Not thinking or feeling it, but *being* it; living it like a second skin.

Many of us hate where we are in our lives, and, sadly, some of us even hate *who* we are. Hate and disdain can be valid and useful emotions. They're packed with energy and can stir one to action. Unfortunately, often these emotions trigger an ingrained fight-or-flight response. This totally natural but difficult to control instinct can send you racing away from life's challenges, or attacking them in an aggressive and unbalanced manner. Despite their raw power, emotions like fear and hate can quickly get in the way of achieving your goals. It's only when you make conscious choices about overcoming challenges that you stand any chance of producing long-term changes to your life.

The Rooms of Your House: Prayer/Meditation Room

The prayer/meditation room represents your spirituality and inner peace. It's a place of quiet introspection. This room is not just about religion—even those who don't claim a particular religious tradition can benefit from spending time being quiet and contemplative each day. This room can be a place where you offer up prayers and positive affirmation for others, as well as express your gratitude for the things in your life.

In the prayer room, you can ask yourself:

- What is my life's purpose?
- How much time do I spend each day in quiet retrospection and gratitude?
- What things in my life I am grateful for?
- Who in my life am I grateful for?
- Who in my life needs prayer and positivity?

Admittedly, taking a long hard look at your life in its current state may not be your idea of a good time, but look closely enough, and you will find something to be grateful for.

There's a well-known Cherokee legend that someone shared with me years ago: a grandfather says to his grandson that he has two wolves fighting within him at all times. One of the wolves is born of anger, hate, fear and jealousy. The other wolf draws its power from peace, love, and kindness. The grandfather explains this same fight is going on inside the boy. The young

Cherokee boy thinks for a moment and then asks, "Which wolf will win?" and the grandfather replies, "The one you feed."

I keep that parable in mind when I'm not feeling, thinking, or behaving at my best. I try to remind myself if I feed the negative feelings, they'll only grow stronger.

It seems unjust that we unconsciously slip into negative emotions so easily, and must work overtime to cultivate positive emotions intentionally, but that's the reality of life as a living, breathing, and feeling human being. It takes *effort* to feel good and cultivate gratitude, but the effort is well worth it.

Exercise: Cultivating Gratitude

This exercise will help you begin to cultivate more gratitude about the current state of your life.

Take the next ten minutes to reflect on, and then write down, *everything* you're grateful for right now. It doesn't matter if it's good, bad, happened yesterday, or twenty years ago. If you're grateful for it, and see it as a stepping stone that has brought you to this point of introspection, write it down.

Starting this journey from a place of gratitude will enable you to move forward with joy and anticipation instead of fear and anxiety. Everything you've endured up to this point, whether you perceive it as good or bad, has led to the realization that your life is ripe for change and transformation. Listen to the voice inside of you whispering you can do more, have more, and be more. Listen closely because it's telling you the truth. You *are* more. You are infinite. You have access to everything you need to live the life of your dreams.

Don't get discouraged if you struggle with this exercise. Practicing gratitude like most things in life, becomes easier the more you do it.

This exercise can become a daily ritual using your Blueprint Gratitude Journal or any journal that you have. Simply jot down thoughts of gratitude at the start or the end of each day. Before long, living gratefully will become so natural you'll notice when you're not being grateful, and you'll consciously make the necessary course corrections.

Exercise: Cultivating Gratitude

I am grateful for/that…

_____

_____

_____

_____

3

THE SEASONS OF LIFE

*"It's not the load that breaks you down,
it's the way you carry it."*

– LENA HORNE

Your life will change. You may feel stuck in a rut, set in your ways, or imprisoned by choices you've made, but it just isn't so. Nothing in this world is static and the only constant is change.

Rather than resent the difficult times, I urge you to lean into them. Life has so much to teach us, and often life's lessons are cloaked in challenge, heartache, and disappointment. I've learned far more about myself during the difficult times in my life than I have in the times of joy and relaxation. When the pressure is off, we tend to be less reflective and evaluative of our lives and the choices we make. When there's money in the bank, our family members are healthy, and we're surrounded by people who value and appreciate us, it feels like springtime in our lives. Unfortunately, there's no such thing as eternal springtime. Life is cyclical, and our life experiences can often reflect nature's four seasons.

Spring – Spring is a time of new beginnings. Things we planted and investments we made last year come into bloom. Meanwhile, we're busy planting a whole new crop that'll hopefully exceed last season's yield. The nights are shorter and the days are longer, and we're able to sit back and enjoy the natural beauty around us, which is fresh and exciting after a long winter. These are the hopeful times in our lives when so much seems possible. It's the beginning of a relationship, the first few months on a new job, or the moment when you finally hit your goal weight after months of clean eating and time at the gym. There's a freshness to these times in our lives that's exhilerating.

Summer – Summer brings with it warmer days, long afternoons, and periods of relaxation maybe in the form of walks in nature, sipping an ice-cold beverage, and swimming in the surf. The ability to rest and recharge we're afforded during the summertime periods in our lives is incredible, but it can be dangerous if we focus only on recreation and fun. When the sun is shining bright and everything in our lives seems to be going well, we must remember to prepare for the autumn and winter seasons that'll eventually come our way. Summer, not unlike Spring, cannot last forever.

Autumn – Autumn brings the harvest along with it. The harvest is when you benefit from the work you've put in during the spring and summer. Any farmer will tell you harvesting the crop is not easy work. It's a stark contrast to the relaxation of spring and summer. It's a time of exertion, but also reaping the rewards that accompany hard work. It's marked by cooler temperatures, trees beginning to give up their leaves, shorter days, and longer nights. If we've been wise about our consumption and how we've used our time during the spring and summer, we'll usually do just fine. Autumn can, however, become difficult for those who were distracted by the beauty of spring and summer and didn't take the time to maintain and store up for the inevitability of fall and winter. These distractions might manifest in a lack of attention to the important relationships in our lives. Or maybe we neglect business and financial matters because the sunshine and flowers seduced us. Many of us know someone who incurred a financial windfall and somehow found themselves financially destitute only a few years later because they forgot springtime is seasonal and must eventually move on.

Winter – In winter, the ground is hard, cold, and not much grows. Nothing we put our hands to seems to work in our favor. The bank says "No" to your new mortgage request. You don't get the job you wanted. A close friend moves away, betrays you or maybe even dies. Divorce, empty nests, weight gain, illness – everywhere you turn, the answer seems to be "no," "not now," or "not ever." It can be even harder to get through these times when you've neglected to store up during spring, summer, and fall. That's why it's so important to be a good steward of your life's resources.

*Being a good steward is having the sense to
plant the seeds and not eat them all.*

STEWARDING YOUR LIFE'S RESOURCES

Financial stewardship is something I had to learn the hard way as a then young wife and mother. I remember the days of "not enough". I remember feeling ashamed when I had to call home and borrow money from my parents. The shame wasn't because I was embarrassed to ask. It was because I knew that I had not properly managed the provisions that I did have. It wasn't until I was in my late 30's that started to take stewardship seriously. One day as I was going over my household budget feeling frustrated because once again I didn't seem to have enough, I started to reflect on the amount of money that had come through my hands since I started working full-time at 19. As the number started to top $500,000, two things occurred to me. In nearly 20 years, I was not without income for more than one year combined and secondly, I was spending way too much money! This is where I came to know for myself that it's not about how much you make but how much you keep.

The universe provides most of us with more than enough to meet our needs in virtually every area of our lives. There is *not* a scarcity of wealth, health, joy, and success out there. The problem is we aren't good stewards when it comes to the provisions we're given and the opportunities we're handed.

How often have you spent too much time in a toxic relationship and then been too tired to give it your all when a great man or woman came along? Remember when you received a large payment and ran right out to buy things you didn't need, only to miss your car or mortgage payment two or three months later? Smoking, excessive drinking, and not exercising seems fun when you're young and healthy; unfortunately, the impact of this behaviour becomes very real when you receive a diagnosis of high blood pressure, diabetes, or cancer later in life.

We've all done it and we continue to do it again and again. We forget our lives are seasonal and cyclical. We get so focused on immediate gratification in the current moment that we don't see the next moment coming right behind it until it slams into us like a runaway train.

I plan to live beyond this moment and I know you do too. As such, the principal lesson the seasons of life teaches us is to appreciate where we are (even though it's not the destination) and to be faithful stewards over the resources we've be given.

All of life is a journey. Regardless of which season you're currently in right now, for better or worse, the others are on their way. Don't fret. Each season brings with it important life lessons.

EXERCISE: ASSESSING CURRENT LIVING ARRANGEMENTS

The following assessment tool is designed to help you evaluate your current living arrangements by rating each area of your life and identifying your unique strengths and areas for improvement.

ASSESS YOUR CURRENT LIVING ARRANGEMENTS						
Ratings: 5=Almost always, **4**=To a great extent, **3**=To some extent, **2**=Rarely, **1**=Not at all		**5**	**4**	**3**	**2**	**1**
KITCHEN	I consume fresh fruits and vegetables each day.					
	I drink at least half my body weight in ounces of water daily to stay hydrated.					
	I eat healthy meals prepared at home at least 4-5 days each week.					
GYM	I exercise 3-4 days a week for at least 30 minutes.					
	I feel good about my overall physical/medical condition.					
	I have a physical exam each year.					
SAFE	I save at least 10% of my earnings as they are received.					
	I contribute a fixed amount to a retirement account each pay period.					
	I have and adhere to a weekly or monthly household budget.					
	I review my income and expenses each quarter to assess financial health.					
DEN	I spend quality time with my family members on a regular basis.					
	I feel the overall quality of my social relationships is good.					
	The balance of giving and receiving in my relationships is good.					
	I express gratitude often for and to those in my life.					
BEDROOM	Each day, I spend time on activities that I find relaxing or recreational.					
	I take at least one vacation annually to focus on myself.					
	I'm satisfied with the overall quality of my sexual well-being and intimacy.					
	I get sufficient sleep each night and wake up feeling refreshed.					
STUDY	I seek out opportunities to learn or do something different.					
	I'm satisfied with my current educational level.					
	I typically stay up-to-date on at least 2-3 topics of interest.					
OFFICE	If money was not an issue, I'd do my job for free.					
	I have created multiple streams of revenue.					
	I feel there are opportunities to advance in my career/field.					
	My earnings are sufficient to meet my family's financial needs.					
PRAYER & MEDITATION ROOM	I spend time each day in quiet reflection, prayer or meditation.					
	I read or listen to positive, uplifting affirmations each day.					
	My overall well-being is better than it was this same time last year.					
	I feel vibrant and happy.					
BATHROOM	I practice releasing any thoughts, feelings, behaviors that aren't useful.					
	I have and apply a process for de-cluttering my home and life.					
	I see myself clearly and I am aware of my strengths and weaknesses.					
	I leverage a trusted counselor or therapist to help me process emotions as needed.					

Once you've completed the assessment, take a moment to appreciate your strengths as well as the areas where things will need to be developed further. The areas or "rooms" where you rated yourself a "4" or "5" are your strengths, and anything less than a "3" might require a bit more reflection and some effort to improve. Remember, no life is without areas that can't stand a little repair. Rooms requiring improvements are just proof that yours is a life that is being lived. Those are the areas you're going to be working to improve going forward.

4

ALWAYS TELL YOURSELF
THE TRUTH

"Trust yourself. Think for yourself. Act for yourself. Speak for yourself. Be yourself."

– MARVA COLLINS

Slowly, your eyes flutter open. You take a deep breath and fill your lungs with the morning air. You stretch out your arms and legs, and feel your body come alive as you push back the covers. It's morning, and long before you drink a cup of warm coffee or tackle that first urgent email, you head to the bathroom.

You look at yourself in the bathroom mirror, evaluate how you look, and determine what you need to do to get yourself prepared for the day to come. In front of the mirror, you brush your teeth and comb your hair, and maybe shave your face (if you're in the face-shaving club), or do your make-up if that's your thing. Long before anyone else sees the version of ourselves we present to the world, *we* see our raw and real selves reflected to us in the bathroom mirror.

The Rooms of Your House:
The Bathroom

The bathroom represents purging and decluttering of your life, including both emotional and physical clutter.

The physical clutter can be obvious in your personal space. Are there random stacks of papers on the kitchen counter or dining room table? Are there boxes everywhere all over the basement or bedroom? Do you have a closet full of clothes you no longer wear? Perhaps you're still holding on to shoes that you can give away?

The bathroom also deals with emotional clutter, including outdated thoughts, beliefs, rituals, and traditions you might be holding on to that are no longer serving you.

The key question to ask yourself when designing the bathroom is:

- What am I holding onto that is no longer useful to me?

In our blueprint metaphor, the bathroom is the place we go to see ourselves honestly and clearly. It's a private space we visit alone. We can be honest, naked, and vulnerable there, and not worry about anyone seeing what we wish to keep private (if we are careful to lock the metaphorical door). When we experience significant challenges in our lives, the bathroom is often where the challenges manifest first. The vulnerability and transparency of the bathroom force us to face the areas in our lives where we haven't made the best choices or wish we'd done things differently. Sometimes the last person we want to be honest with is ourselves, but once we are, every choice we make thereafter can bring us closer to a more fulfilling and purposeful life.

No matter what you might tell or show other people—regardless of the facades you tell yourself you must create—it's important you always tell yourself the truth. Lying to yourself is, at best, unproductive, and at worst, downright destructive.

Unfortunately, this kind of self-honesty gets a bad rap. When what we think we want is warmth and comfort, honesty feels like a cold, wet blanket. It's only a matter of time, however, before the heat of lies and denial turns into the bitter cold realization that you're trapped in an unfulfilling life.

Each new morning gives us the gift of starting anew. Our lives may not be perfect, but if we can honestly assess our circumstances and determine we're moving in the right direction, then we're making progress towards something better. That's what we are looking for: progress, not perfection.

SILENCING THE VOICES

Just as you don't invite strangers into the bathroom to help you look presentable in the mornings, it's important to remember that likewise you don't need to invite them into your private space of reflection. Most of the time, you can look in the mirror and decide for yourself what needs to be done without the distracting advice of others.

Everyone has an opinion, but not all opinions will be useful or helpful.

There are times, however, when welcoming outside guidance from 2-3 trusted friends can be useful. I liken it to going into a fitting room with the 180-degree mirrors. That's enough mirrors to help me see most of myself but not too many so that I walk out feeling overwhelmed and defeated. I'm not sure who came up with the idea of 360-degree mirrors in fitting rooms but whoever it was was probably a size 2. I have a couple of close friends who offer me additional perspectives on what I might not be able to see about myself.

If you have trouble admitting the truth to yourself, the opinions of others can become a helpful resource. If this resonates with you, reach out to a trusted partner, spouse, or friend, and ask: "What do you see that I'm missing?" Just be sure that it's only by explicit invitation that they become a mirror for you.

Of course, our outer appearance is only a small portion of what makes up our whole person. As much as they can offer you reflection, only you can make and commit to the changes necessary in your life.

DECEPTIVE CURB APPEAL

We all know someone who, from outer appearances, seems to have it together. Their life is so impeccably landscaped it reminds you of the finished product on a well-produced renovation and design television program. When you enter the front door of their home, you're impressed by how it looks, feels, and even smells. You smile and think to yourself, "This place is so beautiful. I wish I had this life." That initial spark of inspiration can be useful but keep your eyes open. Things aren't always as they appear. Don't be so quick to sum up their life as perfect.

The longer you stay, and the further into that person's life you venture, the more something else, something *hidden* beneath the surface, may begin to reveal itself. You discover dark and empty rooms with stacks of boxes in the corners. Behind closed doors, you find dust and cobwebs because perhaps no one has been in that room for a long time. You notice things don't quite match up with what you observed from the curb. When the inside of a house doesn't match the outside, it's a clear indication someone is not living authentically.

Living authentically requires you first ask yourself, "What is the truest representation of who I am at this current moment?" The second question authenticity requires we ask is, "Do the interior and exterior of my life line-up? Do they represent who I am becoming and what I believe my purpose is for being alive?"

How would you know if the interior and exterior of your life are in alignment? To begin with, when your lifestyle fits your purpose, you're living authentically. Every room of your dream home should resonate with vibrations of the best and highest version of you (as you imagined in the "Envisioning the Best and Highest Version of Yourself" exercise). If something doesn't fit that vision, it's time to change it or get rid of it. If your current life feels too small, build a bigger one. If your current life seems too big and overwhelming, downsize and focus. Your curb appeal and the inside of your house should complement one another, not be an attempt to deceive people.

EXERCISE – TAKE AN HONEST LOOK

At some point in the next 48 hours, when you're in your bathroom alone, strip down to nothing. (Yes, you need to get totally naked!) Once you're nude, position yourself in front of the mirror and take a couple of minutes to look at yourself.

When I saw myself in the mirror for the first time after losing my hair because of chemotherapy, and felt the shock of seeing the scars on my breasts after surgery, I couldn't help but weep. I allowed myself to cry for a few minutes, but before too long I realized my tears were due to a physical change. Inside, at my core, I was—and still am—the same person I was before chemotherapy. There was also a deeper more fundamental change happening. Cancer was stripping away my vanity. As women, our identities can get tangled up in our physical attributes – our hair and our breasts and cancer came for both.

So as a bid adieu to the vanity that I could perceive in myself in that moment, I acknowledged the strength, gratitude, and courage within me, and realized that nothing that can happen to my physical body will ever change that.

Exercise: Take an Honest Look

When you look in the mirror...

What do you see?

_____

_____

_____

What do you see that you love?

_____

_____

_____

What do you see that can be improved?

_____

_____

_____

What seems out of place?

_____

_____

_____

What things do you love about yourself that you can leverage?

_____

_____

_____

When you do this reflection exercise, don't focus only on aspects of your physical body alone; remember, our journey is about more than the shallowness of curb appeal. Do your best to see your whole and complete self. Carefully observe all that's being reflected physically, spiritually, emotionally, and mentally. It's important we see both the strengths and the areas with opportunity for improvement. There's a place for the optimism of rose-colored glasses, but the bathroom isn't it. The bathroom demands and facilitates honesty and vulnerability. If you lie to yourself in the bathroom, you'll carry those lies into other areas of your life.

5

FOOD, FITNESS AND FINANCES

From my experience working with clients one-on-one and in *The Blueprint* workshops, I've noticed some commonalities in the rooms where most people seem to struggle. These rooms are the more tactical and pragmatic rooms, meaning their function is more physical than emotional, mental, or spiritual. Even still, when these rooms are out of sync with who we are, they can totally derail our lives if we don't tend to them. These are also the rooms that if neglected for too long can not only hinder your ability to develop your dream life but can stop you dead in your tracks. The three rooms are:

- the kitchen, nutrition

- the home gym, fitness

- the safe, finances

I'll explain the safe momentarily, but I'll start with the kitchen and the home gym because they are intimately connected through nutrition, health, and fitness.

In the United States, we see levels of obesity, diabetes, high blood pressure, and chronic disease more prevalent than ever before. The data doesn't lie: as a nation, we make poor nutritional and physical fitness choices. We're making improvements, but we could certainly do better.

The United States of America is also coming out of a recession, so financial concerns are also of great importance to many. People have been laid off and haven't been able to get back to work. Even those with steady jobs sometimes struggle to make ends meet. Perhaps you have friends or family members who must work so many hours they find themselves without the energy, time, or money to exercise or eat healthy. It's an unfortunate and vicious cycle.

If you find yourself struggling in the kitchen, the home gym, and/or the safe, you're not alone, so let's explore how *The Blueprint* can help you redesign these areas so you can experience more ease and joy.

THE KITCHEN AND THE HOME GYM

Three years prior to my cancer diagnosis, I started evaluating the kitchen of my life carefully because it has always been an area of struggle for me.

I come from a southern African-American family. All our important family moments take place around the kitchen table, and almost everything on that table is made with sugar, butter, salt, honey, gravy, cheese and all sorts of unhealthy deliciousness. That was the tradition I was raised in, so when it came time to get my own kitchen in order, I knew I would need to seek advice outside of my immediate family and away from my geographic circle of Southern-fried friends.

I intentionally spoke to people who lived in other parts of the country and were more health-conscious. I spoke to friends who are vegetarians and vegans, and friends who run marathons, exercise consistently and are committed to fitness. I sought their advice and I started paying close attention to what I ate.

The Rooms of Your House:
The Kitchen

The kitchen represents your diet, nutrition, and eating habits. It can also be a place of preparation and service.

In lots of families, the kitchen is a place for intimate family time, where you and your loved ones can gather and catch up on the week's events.

The kitchen is where you want to assess the overall condition of your health and eating habits.

Questions you'll want to ask yourself as you delve into designing the kitchen of your dream home is:

- Do I eat a minimum of three to four servings of fresh, whole fruits and vegetables each day?
- Am I drinking enough water?
- Do I prepare healthy organic meals at home, or am I eating out frequently at fast food restaurants?

I experimented with juicing and supplements, and I tried to get more raw fruits and vegetables into my daily diet. I went through periods of time where I attempted to eliminate sugar and reduce the amount of simple carbohydrates I consumed. As I made these changes to my diet, I felt a lot healthier and lighter. I began to experience all the beautiful feelings and energy that accompany a healthy lifestyle. I started to feel more at home in my body; something I hadn't felt for a really long time. When I received the cancer diagnosis, my body was in better condition to deal with the disease because

I'd begun to focus on my nutrition a few years earlier. I can't know for sure, but I believe if I had continued eating according to the way I'd always eaten throughout my childhood and early adulthood my body would have had a much more difficult time dealing with the side effects of the chemotherapy and radiation. I was able to recover and heal quickly, and I credit nutrition as playing a part in my swift recovery.

We all know how difficult eating healthy can be, but there's no need to become fanatical about it. I didn't make a drastic overhaul to my diet plan. Instead, I made little changes here and there over time. By doing just a few things right, and doing them consistently over time, I got my body in better shape, and I'm so glad I did because it paved the way for me to make future (life-saving) changes. For instance, going through chemotherapy forced me to focus even more on my health. During treatment, certain foods upset my stomach, made me nauseous, and increased my fatigue, so I had to be very careful about what I put in my body. In addition, proper hydration can be an issue during chemo since people often don't feel well, so I had to intentionally drink lots of water, and preferably alkaline water. I learned that if I didn't drink enough water to help flush the toxins out of my body, it could have caused permanent liver and kidney damage, and there's no point in beating cancer only to trade it for liver or kidney disease.

SMALL CHANGES, BIG RESULTS

After I completed treatment and received a clean bill of health, one of my main goals was to maintain the healthy eating habits I'd developed prior to and during my treatment. But, like most things in life, that was easier said than done.

While undergoing chemo, my taste buds stopped operating as usual, and everything started to taste like metal. Food I used to love didn't taste good anymore, and I no longer craved sugar. (I never thought I'd experience a time in my life when vanilla cake with cream cheese frosting didn't taste divine, but I *did*!) This made it easier for me to eat food that was high in nutritional value because I saw the food as fuel for my body to repair itself. Once I started flushing the chemo out of my body, however, it was as if someone had flipped a switch. One morning, I woke up and all I wanted were cakes, cookies, and pies!

Today, I balance these cravings and the need to eat healthy with the same technique I used prior to the cancer treatment: once again, I committed to making small changes over time, and I would urge you to do the same.

We love to drink sweetened ice tea in the South. It's even referred to at an iconic Atlanta restaurant as the "Table Wine of the South". We take our sweet tea very seriously here. One of the small changes I made was to start drinking unsweetened ice tea with a drop or two of Stevia, a natural sweetener that doesn't spike insulin the way refined sugar does. Another simple and delicious change I made was to add lemon to my water. Lemon helps alkalize the body. Research suggests that disease flourishes in a person whose system is overly acidic. Our modern diet often leads to a very acidic state, so I put lemon in my water to help combat the acidity. Not only does the lemon have a positive impact, but it also makes the water taste better, so I'm likely to drink more of it. I'm also more likely to choose water over less healthy alternatives such as juice or soda because I know the water is helping me flush out toxins and keep my body in balance. Dropping a piece of lemon into your water isn't a big deal, but it's one of those small changes that can have a big impact on your health over time.

Based on my observation, through traveling across the country and working with clients from coast to coast, it seems that in the United States, we're far too passive about our diets. We eat what we have always eaten, or whatever is put in front of us, and we rarely consider the long-term consequences on our health. If the kitchen is one of the areas you struggle with, you'll need to become a much more conscious eater. A food journal can help because, much like a gratitude journal, we pay a lot more attention to what we eat when we write it down. Never are the negative impacts of our westernized, fast-food life style more obvious than when I travel internationally. In other countries, fresh fruits and vegetables along with healthier preparation techniques like grilling, broiling and steaming are much more widely used than here in the United States.

I'm not a health professional, so I encourage you to talk to your doctor or nutritionist about what will work best for you. It could be something as simple as taking a multivitamin or getting more exercise and more sleep. The point is to pay attention to your body, how it responds to what you are putting inside of it, and how you are treating it.

You're going to want your body in optimum condition when you tackle the changes you're making in your life. It's difficult to address finances, relationships, and the other aspects of your life if you are not feeling healthy and energized. Regardless of what your dream home looks like, it almost certainly includes a kitchen stocked with healthy food and a well-used home gym.

The Home Gym

Hand in hand with the kitchen is the home gym which addresses our need for physical movement. Even if you succeed in having a pretty healthy diet, your overall health and wellness can suffer if you don't get adequate exercise.

Most personal trainers and fitness experts suggest exercising at least 3-5 times per week for 30-45 minutes. While there are hundreds of new tools and apps that make it easier to track and analyze our fitness routines, many people (myself included) complain that we simply can't find the time to exercise consistently. Setting a goal, like running in a 5K, and finding a partner who will work on it with you and hold you accountable can be a good technique. Hiring a personal trainer might also be another way to jumpstart your efforts. Living a life **of** purpose requires living **on** purpose. Remind yourself that living your dreams will be much more rewarding if your body is healthy.

**The Rooms of Your House:
The Safe**

The safe represents your personal finances – everything from your income, debt, investments, retirement savings, and emergency fund.

The safe also deals with your feelings and habits about money. Financial stability represents safety and security for many people.

The question you need to ask here is:

- What is my net worth? (If you don't have the information to figure that out, then you probably need to spend some time focusing on the safe.)
- Am a carrying too much debt?
- Am I living within my means?
- Are there areas where I could reduce spending?
- Am I planning for my financial future?
- Do I have a will and/or living trust?

THE SAFE

When the doctor informed me I had breast cancer, all I could think was, "Am I going to be able to keep working?"

I *needed* to keep working, at least a little bit, to have enough money to cover my family's living expenses. I'm a single mom with two children; my oldest is finishing college, and my youngest is in grade school and still lives at home with me. I'm self-employed, so if I don't work, I don't invoice . . . and that means I can't pay my bills.

Getting the cancer diagnosis forced me to take a serious look at my overall finances and spending habits. For my family to financially survive my illness, it became necessary to cut out all excess expenses wherever possible.

An example of this is that we had to eliminate our family summer vacation, though I told my youngest son it was only temporarily. When I received the cancer diagnosis, I knew we wouldn't be able to go anywhere for vacation that year. It wasn't just because I was dealing with the treatment; it was because I couldn't afford the financial risk of going on vacation when I didn't know if I was going to be able to work enough to ensure our bills would be paid in the months to come. That was a very scary feeling.

As a family, we looked at what could be cut away. We asked ourselves, "What are we paying for that we don't absolutely need?" We turned the cable off and watched DVDs instead, and we looked for other opportunities to cut expenses and save money. No one likes to pinch pennies or deny themselves luxuries they feel they've worked hard to obtain, but it's important to remember that often a dream life involves letting go of things. When money gets tight, it can be an excellent reminder that quality of life is much more important than all the *stuff* we think we need, or that we've accumulated over time.

When you're looking at the challenges in your life, your finances, just like health and nutrition, are of primary importance because they impact all the other areas of your life. You are probably familiar with Abraham Maslow's theory of the human hierarchy of needs. Usually represented as a pyramid, Maslow argued human needs flow from physiological, to safety, to love/belonging, to esteem, before peaking at self-actualization. Everyone would like to be at the top of that pyramid, but if you don't have food, clothing, shelter, and a sense of safety, you can't get close to becoming your best self. You'll be too busy trying to figure out how you are going to get your next meal. That's why keeping a close eye on your Safe is so important.

Exercise – Simple Changes

Simple changes can often be the most effective when it comes to managing the three rooms that address our nutrition, fitness, and finances. Use the exercise below to identify small changes you can implement immediately to improve the Kitchen, Home Gym, and Safe.

Start today! Write down the date you will begin implementing the changes above and then share that plan with a trusted friend or family member to help hold you accountable. Be sure to include a plan that includes the help and support you will need from others which is an important element if any change is to be sustained. Make an action to evaluate your progress over the next 30, 60 and 90 days to see how you're doing.

Exercise 5.1 – Simple Changes

What are three changes I can implement to improve my nutrition?

1. _____

2. _____

3. _____

What are three changes I can make to improve my overall physical fitness?

1. _____

2. _____

3. _____

What are three ways I can reduce expenses and increase savings?

1. _____

2. _____

3. _____

6

BELIEVING IS SEEING

*"'I can't' are two words that have never
been in my vocabulary. I believe in me
more than anything in this world."*

— WILMA RUDOLPH

It's time to break ground on your construction project. Breaking ground is symbolic of moving from the conceptual phase into something more material. You're the architect of this project, but you're also the general contractor who organizes the day to day grunt work. Beyond just dreaming and planning, you must show and lay the bricks one at a time that build the walls of your new home. When those first beads of sweat drip down your forehead, you'll know its time to start making difficult choices and sacrifices. Building your dream life must go from something on a page to something tangible. Often that means tedious and unglamorous work. It's time to get your hands dirty.

We all must do the work without reward or acknowledgment, and we'll have to do it for a long time. It takes months before a house or building begins to look like the final structure, so don't be disappointed if your life doesn't change drastically right away. Savor every small step along the road because delays and detours are inevitable.

As you well know by now, my love for home renovation shows runs deep because I see so many parallels to life, and especially to this process you're walking through right now in this book. It's those weather delays, shortages of skilled workers, budget constraints, unavailable raw materials, and unplanned changes to the blueprints that keep my eyes glued to the television screen. Of course, your detour won't get resolved by the time the credits roll the way they do in the show, but you can rest in knowing that resolution always comes, one way or another. Try to enjoy the unexpected detours in your life in the way you'd enjoy them on-screen, knowing that sooner than later, the dust will settle.

The Rooms of Your House:
The Bedroom

The bedroom is all about you. It represents your private sanctuary, a place of rest, relaxation, and renewal.

The overall condition of the bedroom can also represent your primary romantic relationship and aspects of your sexuality.

Key questions in the bedroom include:

- How would I rate my overall level of well-being?
- Am I getting enough rest?
- Do I have ways to renew and recharge my emotional batteries?
- Am I happy with the state of my sex life?

Before you can make anyone else a believer in your goals, hopes, and dreams, you'll have to be the first one to believe. Thought leaders, athletes, and artists have long touted the power of visualization and belief. As American industrialist and founder of Ford Motor Company, Henry Ford, famously said, "Whether you think you can, or you think you can't – you're right." The largest obstacle standing between you and what you want to achieve is your own mind.

Picture the dream home we've been discussing for many chapters now. Do you honestly believe you can attain that life and live in that home? You won't achieve it until you believe it. What you can and cannot attain is defined by only one person: you.

The person who says it cannot be done should not interrupt the person doing it. Chinese Proverb

Throughout the years, I've observed that we spend far too much energy convincing ourselves that things are impossible or can't be done when history shows us the opposite. The people who achieve great things are the ones who overcome limiting beliefs and actively strive for the seemingly—and otherwise thought-to-be—impossible.

It was a long-held and commonly acknowledged belief that running a mile in under four minutes was a human impossibility, until Roger Bannister did just that in 1954. Once Bannister paved the way, dozens of other runners broke the four-minute barrier in the months that followed. As it turned out, it wasn't a physical obstacle that prevented athletes from running that fast; it was a mental barrier, or to put it another way, a limiting belief.

The once thought "impossible" four-minute mile is now considered a standard pace for male middle-distance runners.

What limiting beliefs might you be able to smash through the same way Bannister did?

What impossible things can you accomplish?

STAYING FLEXIBLE

The everyday roles of being a spouse, an employee, and/or a parent can send your life's journey off its intended track. I know it did mine. I got married at 18 years old and had my first baby by the time I was 21. At a relatively young age, my life became all about making sure someone else could have her dreams instead of me defining and pursuing my own.

As a wife and a parent, my purpose was intimately intertwined with that of my child and husband at the time. I've observed it consistently with friends and clients, as well, after they become spouses and parents. You can't think only about yourself anymore, and it becomes easy to let responsibilities take over your life, especially if the practice of self-care wasn't part of your upbringing.

As a young wife and mother, I started to feel guilty if I even tried to do something for myself, and whether the circumstances around your detours are like mine, the result is the same: you put yourself last.

What about that thing you always wanted to do? What about going back to school? What about starting that business you always wanted to build or writing that book?

Once you're a parent, a little voice inside starts answering these questions by saying, "You can't take money from the budget to do something like that. That's just irresponsible. You have to think about your children going to college someday, not your dreams."

Today, I have a 27-year-old daughter, and, to be honest, I'm glad she hasn't married yet. I tell her all the time I'm proud that she made different life choices than I did. I'm certainly not against marriage or having babies, but by delaying marriage and motherhood, my daughter has opened up possibilities in her life that were not available to me in my twenties. Now I understand that it's due to the nature of our self-talk and what we start to tell ourselves once we are responsible for another life. The messages of selfless sacrifice for others that is inherited by many young girls gets reinforced in our subconscious mind before we're even old enough to imagine different lives than our mothers lived.

We're looking for progress, not perfection on our journeys, so detours are useful and can even be considered part of The Plan. In fact, you may be surprised to find the twists and turns in the road ultimately define what you want to achieve. Many parents never realize how important family is going to be to them until they're holding a baby in their arms. Then, suddenly, family becomes the foundation to their life's' blueprint.

That's why we create our blueprints in pencil. We'll have to change and adapt along the way. The indominable belief in the vision you have for your life and showing up to do the work is what will ensure your progress.

Motherhood is one of the great blessings in my life and I have much respect for those of us who share, by birthing biological children or through adoption, in the honor of helping to nurture and shape future generations. I equally respect and appreciate women like Oprah Winfrey, Ellen DeGeneres, Regina Hall, Cameron Diaz, Tracee Ellis Ross and my daughter who give themselves permission to dream a different dream and who choose to delay motherhood or choose a different kind of maternal legacy altogether.

Take a few moments to recall the image of yourself in the mirror from our exercise earlier in the book; not the physical image you saw in the mirror, but the emotional, spiritual and mental reflections.

Ask yourself these questions:

- What is keeping me from living my life on purpose?

- When did I give up on pursuing my dreams and what where the circumstances surrounding that decision?

- What hard truths haven't I acknowledged about my lack of intention, effort or both to live out my dreams?

Before moving into a new home, people will often walk around inside the new house while it's still empty to experience the space and solidify the belief that it'll be their home someday. That's what I'm asking you to do right now.

Go to your bedroom and picture yourself walking around in your new life. A life that fits you, a life custom designed by you and for you. Walk around and see what it would feel like to really be you in that new life, living the best and highest version of yourself. Get comfortable with it. Touch the walls and experience the space. Identify where the light switches are and what the floors look like. Use this simple metaphor to help visualize your life as custom designed home, each room reflecting the best version of your life in that area of life.

When you do this exercise, at some point you're going to feel a smile spread across your face. You might even let out a sigh of relief with the realization that, "Yes, this is my life. I can have this. I can do this. I can be the best, highest version of myself."

This experience will be a blessing. You will be encouraged and excited as you walk away from this activity and feel a new sense of energy around your transformative journey.

EXERCISE – REFRAMING YOUR STORY

Look in the mirror and repeat this to yourself everyday. You can also affirm all or parts of it to yourself throughout the day.

Affirmation

You, _____, can accomplish your goals and live your dream life. You are strong enough, courageous enough and capable enough to undertake the journey of living a life of authenticity and purpose. There are limitless possibilities available to help you achieve your goals and you're open to them. You draw the most effective and innovative ideas to you. If you make mistakes, you will use those failures as opportunities to learn and do it better the next time. You don't fear failure. It's part of the process. You aren't overly concerned with or distracted by naysayers and haters. Their words have zero influence over your ability to succeed. You are not constrained by time because you realize that the Universe can conspire with you to manifest your dreams at warp speed.

You are worthy and deserve to live a fulfilling and joyful life.

_____

Signature

7

ASSEMBLE YOUR DREAM TEAM

*"Surround yourself with only people who
are going to lift you higher."*

— OPRAH WINFREY

When I think about the impromptu dance parties and multiple movie nights experienced in my den among my family and friends, I think about the laughter and support and warmth that fills the air in that room. These people are my personal Dream Team.

Up until this point in the book, I've emphasized the need to focus on your own voice and vision for your life. While that remains essentials throughout the process of developing your Blueprint, it's now time to acknowledge that you're going to need a support system if you're going to sustain any positive life changes you've made or intend to make. No one goes through life alone. The decisions we make and the actions we take have a ripple effect, and the special people in your life who fill your "Den" with laughter and smiles can be instrumental in helping or hindering your progress.

Not everyone has a support network in place with family and friends. If that is your situation, you might think you have to go it alone. If you feel like you're alone in the world and that no one is there to support you, I urge you to recognize we're all connected to a Source of unlimited and inexhaustible support. You're stronger than you think, and you have more resources at your disposal than you realize. Look within yourself and you'll find a deep well of energy that will never run dry. When you feel alone in the world, draw upon that energy from within. You'll be amazed at what you can accomplish.

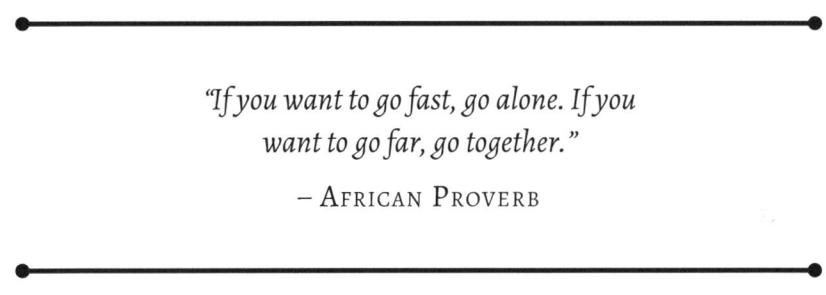

"If you want to go fast, go alone. If you want to go far, go together."

– AFRICAN PROVERB

DREAMS REQUIRE COMMUNITY

An architect doesn't build a house all on her own. A team of masons, electricians, carpenters, plumbers, and a plethora of other specialized technicians bring their expertise to a construction or renovation project.

That's why, when I host my live *Blueprint* events across the country, I don't do them alone. I've put together what I call my "dream team" – a group of nutritionists, relationship coaches, life coaches, financial advisers, fitness experts, and others who have agreed to work with me to share their knowledge and wisdom regarding the areas of self-improvement in which they are well versed.

As someone doing this work by way of this book, you will need to form your own dream team. You'll want to identify people and resources that can help you address the rooms in your house that need improvement, alignment or both. Your dream team doesn't have to be made up of leading experts or famous gurus. It can simply be someone in your life who has mastered the area you're trying to improve, be it managing money, maintaining healthy relationships, building a successful business or career, staying in shape, or being spiritually well-attuned. When you have these individuals identified, they represent resources you can tap into for council and advice when you get stuck.

If personal friendships and support are something you don't currently have, but know will be necessary to reach your goals, you'll need to actively seek them out. The internet provides access to a global community you can leverage. There are many people embarking on similar life changes and transformations. Others have already gone through these changes successfully and will be eager to share advice and encouragement.

There's a secret to developing lasting relationships. When you approach relationship development from the perspective of "what can I do to support this person?" rather than "what can this person do to assist me?", the natural outcome is a village of people who want to help you achieve your goals. Look for opportunities to provide value and assistance to others. Share what you know or simply offer a non-judgemental ear. Sometimes the most profound service we can provide is just to listen. Build a network of relationships by providing value, and, when the time comes to ask for help, you'll be surprised at the number of people who will step forward and assist you.

EXERCISE: DRAFT YOUR DREAM TEAM

Use the table below to identify people in your life who you can draft for your dream team. Remember, your dream team members can be well-known experts with lots of resources like books, podcasts, or blogs, and videos available to help you, or they can simply be friends you've known for years who have always cooked healthy meals and would be happy to share recipes and cooking tips with you.

Exercise: Draft Your Dream Team	
Room	Names of Potential Dream Team Members
Kitchen	
Gym	
Safe	
Den	
Bedroom	
Study	
Office	
Prayer & Meditation Room	
Bathroom	
Kitchen	

If you already have an established network of friends and family, somewhere along your journey the people close to you are going to notice that you're outgrowing your current life. Unfortunately, this may trigger a fear of loss among some of them.

Perhaps there was a time during your youth when a best friend moved out of the neighborhood. Maybe her parents got a better job and purchased a bigger house across town. Do you remember how you felt? Were you terrified you'd never see your friend again? Well, that fear is *exactly* how some people in your life may begin to feel when they see you starting to shift gears or move in an entirely different direction.

When they observe you're taking a jack-hammer to your existing foundational beliefs – beliefs you likely shared with them – they may feel like they're losing a friend. They may even believe your desire to improve your life is a direct criticism of how they are living their lives.

The Rooms of Your House:
The Den

The den represents your overall relationships with family and friends.

The den is also a place where friends and family can gather to socialize. It represents fun and fellowship.

Questions you should consider when contemplating your den include:

- How satisfied am I with the overall state of my relationships?
- Am I spending quality time with those who are most important in my life?
- Am I holding onto toxic relationships?

Some people have the maturity and skills to express how they feel in these circumstances, but many do not. Those unable to articulate their feelings – even if they are coming from a place of love – may show their fear of loss in the form of jealousy, judgment, or outright resentment.

"Who does she think she is?" "That's too much 'house' for him." "She always did think she was better than everyone else." "I don't think you should do it. What if it doesn't work out?" These are just a few of the feelings you may have to navigate and oftentimes coming from people who have known and even loved you for years. When the quality of relationships hasn't been evaluated, and clear channels of communication haven't been established, relationships in your life can begin to breakdown and become potential roadblocks along your journey.

Evaluating the quality of relationships is important because the stress of change will impact those closest to you. Sometimes even second and third-degree connections you never considered will be impacted by your changes.

Remember our example of a childhood friend moving away? It's unlikely your friend's parents took your feelings into account when making the move, but your life was undoubtedly touched by their decision. Maybe your parents needed to comfort you or take time to schedule and drive you to play dates across town. Your parents were therefore impacted as well. Don't underestimate just how many lives you've touched. You probably have more important relationships in your life than you realize, so take the necessary time to evaluate their status.

Meaningful relationships need to be at their healthiest if they're going to withstand the demands and stressors of transformational change.

Meaningful relationships need to be at their healthiest if they're going to withstand the stress of transformational change. Make every effort to ensure the people in your support network feel valued and appreciated by you, and vice versa. Give them the courtesy of a "heads-up" that you intend to make changes to your life and you'll need their support. This support can be anything from small and seemingly insignificant contributions to large and highly active involvement.

While a quick review of your social media feed on any given day may leave you with the impression the world is collapsing, and most people are selfish and only interested in what impacts them directly, when you ask for help you'll discover a true and endless bounty of human generosity. People are good, and they like to help others succeed if they can. Don't give in to the seemingly endless cynicism and darkness the media feeds on. Interact with people and you'll

ASK FOR WHAT YOU NEED

In my work consulting with corporations and coaching executives, I help implement large-scale organizational changes. In their research on Effective Change Management, CEB Gartner cites that "60% of big, structural changes end in failure and consequent losses in revenue, productivity, and competitiveness." All good change management methodologies require a communications strategy and plan to ensure success of any transformational change. One of the first activities of most communications strategies is to complete a stakeholder analysis. It's the process of identifying all the people who will be impacted by a change and then meeting with them to gather requirements and discuss how to best help them move from the current state to the future state. Some stakeholders will be heavily involved in implementing the change while others may only need a high-level explanation. The goal of the stakeholder analysis is to gather the necessary information to ensure we are providing relevant and timely information and training to help them perform in the future. Not only does this approach work well for organizational transformation but I've also helped my coaching clients find great success using a similar approach in their personal transformations.

Clear and frequent communication is what can make or break the success of big, sometimes sweeping, initiatives involving large numbers of employees. Employees must be informed about a few key aspects of the change itself:

- What's changing,

- why it's critical to the long-term success of
  the organization,

- who will be involved,

- the timeline, and

- how the proposed changes will impact the organization's expectations of them before, during, and
  after implementation.

In the same way a corporation monitors how each department is han-
dling the changes, you also need to keep an eye on how your friends and
family are responding to your changes. In the absence of frequent communication, the people in your life will become frustrated as they try to figure out
what role they should play in your new and expanding life. If you can be clear
about what you need, why you need it, how they can support you differently
than in the past, , and when you'll need their assistance, you'll be more likely
to get the support you require to make and maintain lasting change in your
life. When building your blueprint, it's important to identify the impact of
your changes on "stakeholders' in your life and be clear regarding the level of
involvement you'd like them to have in your personal transformation.

Sometimes support will come from the most surprising places. Often,
it's those we least expect who end up offering us a helping hand. Some people
will want to be cheerleaders and supporters for you. They'll want to be inte-
gral to your growth and development by providing ongoing support, encouragement, and accountability. At the same time, you'll sometimes see a lack of
support from the people you most expected it. This can be disappointing, but
not everyone wants to sit next to you in the co-pilot seat while you transform
your life before their eyes. For some, it's easier to sit on the sidelines with a
"call me when it's over" attitude, and there isn't anything wrong with that.
What's important is that you communicate your intentions clearly so that

those in your life will be informed, regardless of whether they're actively participating or holding their breath in the bleachers.

As a parent, I've learned just how import clear communication is when providing support to my children. When I sit down to talk with my adult daughter, I try to remember to ask, "Do you want me to listen? Do you want me to problem-solve with you, or do you want me to fix the problem? Let me know what level of involvement you want from me." I've learned to do this because, as a mother, my default mode is to get in there and fix it. Truth be told, I do that sometimes even when it's not my children. But my daughter is an adult and she doesn't need me to fix everything for her anymore. That's why I make an effort to get clarity on whether she's looking for help with a problem, wants advice, or just wants to vent some frustration.

If you can instruct those on your dream team how you need them to show up for you, you'll all share the benefits that come from deepening friendships built on trust and vulnerability which will help you appreciate the good times and get you through the difficult ones.

EXERCISE: ALL FEEDBACK IS A GIFT

Look back at the self-assessment exercise in Chapter 3. How did you rate yourself in the den? It's time to expand on that assessment. Self-analysis is of critical importance, but when it comes to assessing the status of relationships, it's equally important that you get an outside point of view.

This exercise involves asking the people how they would rate the overall quality of your relationship with them. Keep in mind this exercise need not be a one-time thing. This sort of relationship-based feedback can and should be explored on an ongoing basis.

When seeking feedback, don't just ask the people who love you and think you're great. You'll also want to call up the courage to seek feedback from people you find challenging, harsh, or contentious to be around. This can be intimidating, but try to approach all the feedback you receive as a gift.

Try to get down to the nitty-gritty of what they're trying to communicate. There's an excellent chance you'll learn something important about yourself in the process.

That said, every village has its idiot. These are the people who feed on drama, constantly argue trivialities, and would love an opportunity to tell you what they "really" think about you. Don't give them the opportunity. Much like the internet trolls we all come across online, these folks are more concerned with hearing their own voice and stirring up trouble than they are acknowledging anything close to reality. Use your best judgement and avoid the village idiot when possible.

It's the people who know you best who will likely have the most applicable and actionable feedback, so make sure you talk with your parents, children, spouse, partner, and closest friends. In the workplace setting, you'll want to talk with anyone who reports to you, a couple of peers and your direct manager or supervisor.

Another tip is to try and make sure people are in a good place mentally when you engage in this discussion. Choose the time and setting carefully. (Immediately after you've had an argument, or the car has broken down probably isn't the best time to analyze a relationship!)

Remain open to feedback throughout these discussions. Your initial response will almost certainly be defensive, especially if the person expresses criticism of the relationship. It's our instinct to defend ourselves, so you may find yourself wanting to say, "Oh, no. That's not what's going on. Here's my reason for that." Try to hold off on this impulse. You're seeking their perspective, their sense of reality regarding the quality of your relationship. You can always evaluate it later by comparing it to other feedback you've received and then decide to accept or toss it. You aren't trying to persuade them to see it like you do. If you get defensive or argumentative, you aren't going to get the information you're looking for. Openness and vulnerability are critical if you're going to improve the significant relationships in your life.

Exercise – All Feedback Is A Gift

Questions to ask during individual feedback sessions:

How would you rate the overall quality of our relationship on a scale of 1-5?

Ratings: 5=Excellent, 4=Great, 3=Amicable, 2=Needs Work, 1=Difficult	5	4	3	2	1

In what ways does our relationship positively impact your life?

_____

_____

_____

In what ways does our relationship challenge or frustrate you?

_____

_____

_____

What are one or two things I could do to improve the quality of our relationship?

_____

_____

_____

8

LEGACY

"Greatness occurs when your children love you, when your critics respect you and when you have peace of mind."

– QUINCY JONES

By this point in the book, you've already developed many elements of a blueprint for your future life, but now it's time to boil that vision down to a specific vision statement. Perhaps you've already created a vision statement for yourself while participating in a vision board party, a training event or workshop. If you have, that's fantastic! In this chapter I'm going to urge you to return to that work and revise your vision statement based on new insights that you've gained from reading this book.

The simple approach to developing a vision statement involves fast-forwarding 15-20 years into the future and then looking back over your life to this point in time. For example, your 35-year-old-self would fast-forward to your imagined version of your 55-year-old-self, turn around, look back on your life and breath a sigh of appreciation at all you've accomplished. In that positive mental and emotional space of gratitude, ask yourself this question "what were the 1-2 critical changes that I made in each area of my life twenty years ago that are most responsible for getting me here?" In other words, what actions did you take that you feel most contributed to living the life of your dreams. Once you can answer that question, you can begin to build a blueprint for how to get there. You might want to look out 40 or 50 years as well. Regardless of how far into the future you choose to look, make sure that your plan to get there has annual milestones so that you can easily chart your effort and progress.

Your Personal Vision Statement

I've often found the people who live the most purposeful, happy, and joyous lives are those who live a life of service to others. That's why a compelling personal vision statement should include your overall contribution to a larger community, or to humanity.

If you want to live an extraordinary life, if you believe you're destined to live a life of purpose and authenticity (and I *know* you are!) there must be a cause that you support you're your life. There must be something bigger than just personal success, fame, or wealth. Extraordinary individuals contribute to the world at large. It's part of their life's work. They may not start out with such grandiose ideas but ultimately a life of real purpose ripples throughout a family, a community and maybe even the world.

"I equip and inspire individuals to embrace the purposeful and authentic lives they were meant to live." Trellis Usher

How might you improve the world around you? What is your contribution going to be? What legacy will you leave to your family and community?

If you don't align your life's purpose to a higher calling, there's a good chance you won't stick with the journey for the long-haul. Life is wrought with distractions, some valid and important and some petty and insignificant. You'll experience doubt and fear, so there must be something pulling you along and calling you to continue to move forward despite other things competing for your time.

Many people approach the acquisition of wealth as their singular focus regarding legacy. This is usually a mistake, because money is not what they're truly after. What they're seeking – what, I might be so bold as to argue is what we're *all* seeking – is the freedom, purpose, community, and recognition we associate with wealth.

On the day you leave this earth, you won't take any of your material wealth with you. Few people will care how many cars were parked in their garage or how big their house was. What they'll care about is how many lives they touched and how you impacted the world for the betterment of others.

Sometimes having an impact on the world means doing or creating something that helps thousands of people. More often, however, the biggest impacts are made at the person-to-person level. If you were lucky enough to have a cherished grandparent, a teacher who helped you when your confidence was failing, or a mentor who reached out a hand and provided support during a difficult period in your life, you already know the people who transform our lives are rarely the ones you read about in the newspaper or see on television or the internet.

You don't have to be Melinda Gates or Barack Obama to leave a legacy. To some individuals and communities, your legacy will mean more than those big names ever could.

If you want to change the world for the better, start by offering help to your existing network. We all want to make a big splash in the world, but it's within the close-knit circle of your family, friends, and mentors that we can have make the most life-altering impacts.

If, one hundred years from now, I were able to look back and see the legacy I left behind, I would want it to be that I helped people live more joyful and authentic lives. I want to have helped people give themselves permission to remove the limits and pursue the lives they're meant to live. If I can help people to do that, I'll be a happy woman. I will have created the legacy I intended to leave behind.

Keeping that in mind, I try to ensure most of what I do supports that vision. Whether it's my life and leadership coaching or my corporate consulting, I strive to inspire people, and provide them with tools that encourage them to think about their lives and their careers differently.

My goal is to move people away from listening to all the cynicism. I want people to dream. I want people to get excited about the aspects of their lives they've been told are unrealistic, foolish endeavours, or that "don't pay enough." I say, be unrealistic. Be foolish. Dream, my friend, dream!

We spend so much time doing the practical things life requires of us. We must put food on the table. If we've chosen a life partner, we have those responsibilities and obligations. If we have children, we must be parents to our kids. We must go to work and earn a decent living. But that doesn't mean we have to give up on our hopes and dreams. Your legacy is tied to your vision, and your vision should be aligned with your hopes and dreams; but hopes and dreams on their own aren't enough to make tangible and significant changes in your life.

When I begin a coaching engagement with a client, many of them can clearly articulate what they believe their purpose is. And yet when I review their calendars and to-do lists, there isn't a single thing on them that's going to move them any closer to achieving what they want from life. Their lists are filled with, "Pick-up groceries," "Drop the kids off at school," and "File the taxes" – all the practical tasks that must be completed. They haven't prioritized anything that brings them joy or is part of their legacy. If you'd look at these people from the outside, they have all the trappings of success but still feel stuck on a hamster wheel of responsibilities and obligations. They're very smart, capable individuals but haven't figured out how to navigate the change from obligation to purpose.

Somewhere along the way, we stop asking ourselves the important questions: What is my life all about? What brings me joy? What makes me happy? What am I here to do? And if you're one of the lucky ones who already has a defined vision statement for your life, your questions should be centered around how much progress you are or are not making. Are you getting lazy? Have you allowed yourself to become distracted by unproductive activities and habits? Do recent life changes require you to revise your vision statement? Applying inquiry and probing questions will help keep you on track.

EXERCISE: DEFINING YOUR LEGACY

Go back and edit your current vision statement, or, if you're writing your vision statement for the first time, begin with the end state in mind.

Remember, it needs to include your larger contribution to humanity. You have the power within you to change the world, so don't play small with your dreams. I want you to dream as big as the sky is wide!

What would your life or legacy look like if you were able to look back on it once you are no longer here? What product or service did you create or master? What individual or group directly benefited from your personal contribution? What positive imprint did you make on humanity? We often have a vague sense of what we want our legacy to be, but by writing it down, we're forced not only to clearly articulate it, but also to embrace it as a real thing, a possible future instead of just an idea floating around in our heads.

Exercise – Defining Your Legacy
My Legacy

What will my contribution(s) be?

Who will benefit directly and indirectly from my contribution(s)?

9

TAKING ACTION, PART 1 –
SETTING GOALS

"The journey of 1000 miles begins with a single step."

– LAO TZU

As with any construction project, the building of your dream home requires you to take action toward the final goal.

Goal setting is different from the vision work you've been doing up until now. Goal setting provides the tactical plan-of-action. It allows you to set targets, measure progress, and adjust your course accordingly.

Keep in mind you're never stuck. You can always adjust your goals or add new ones. You'll just need to balance the addition new goals with accountability for your initial ones. Don't give in to the desire to change your goals whenever life becomes challenging. Remember, you're in it for the long haul. Rome wasn't built in a day and lives don't transform over night. When life throws a curve ball your way, adjust but don't use that as an opportunity to give up.

Be Specific

To begin your goal setting process, go back and review your Current Living Arrangements Assessment in Chapter 3. The assessment tool was designed to help you prioritize the areas where you're experiencing the most challenges in your life. As such, you'll probably want to begin the goal setting process by focusing on those rooms.

For example, if the Home Gym came up as an area of opportunity for you, you'll want to establish some health and fitness goals.

Something like, "I just want to exercise more," is an ineffective goal. You can't develop a plan around a target like that because it's not precise. What does "exercise more" mean exactly? How will you know when you've been successful? How do you define "more"? Heck, how do you define "exercise"?

A better goal in the Home Gym area of your house would be, "I am going to do 30 minutes of cardio twice a week along with an additional 30 minutes of strength training once a week." That goal is specific, it's measurable, it's realistic, and it's time-bound. You need to be *that* specific with your goal setting.

Defining which days and times of the week you'll be completing your tasks might be especially effective if you have a hectic schedule or family commitments to balance with your desired activities around self-improvement. Create a calendar and schedule in the activities most important to your transformation to ensure they get done.

Remember, specificity is everything when it comes to goal setting. If the Safe (personal finance) was a room you needed to focus on in your assessment, simply saying, "I need to create a budget," or "I need to save more money," is not going to cut it. You need to set a goal such as, "I will save [X] percentage/[X] dollars from my paycheck every week for the next nine months." That level of specificity allows you to hold yourself accountable and accurately measure your progress.

S.M.A.R.T. Goals

S.M.A.R.T. is a mnemonic acronym that project managers began using about thirty years ago to establish practical objectives and goals for teams and projects. It is still widely used today in organizations and I also use it in my coaching work with executive leaders. This approach to goal setting is just as useful when it comes to personal transformation.

Here's how the acronym breaks down:

Specific – It's far too easy to be general about what we want to achieve when it comes to self-improvement. Regardless of your goals – whether they involve making more money, getting in better shape, or improving your relationships – specificity regarding what you want to achieve is of vital importance. Not only does specificity encourage focus, it also prevents overwhelm, supports practicality, and facilitates development of plans outlining action-steps in specific areas.

Measurable – Knowing whether you're making progress towards your goals allows you to maintain momentum when things are going well, as we as implement course corrections when things aren't working the way you anticipated. If you don't measure your progress, you'll have no idea what's working and what isn't. Goals that involve specific numeric values – "I want to lose ten pounds," or "I want to eliminate $1,000 of credit card debt," – provide key indicators that allow you to measure progress towards a desired end state.

Assignable – Who is going to be performing the specific tasks necessary to achieve your goals? When implementing S.M.A.R.T. goal setting in a team environment, everyone needs to be clear regarding who is assigned with what task, and how those actions contribute to the overall objectives of the project. When the project in question is your own life, responsibility for completing most of the tasks will fall squarely on your shoulders.

Realistic – This is where goal-setting can get off-track. There's a very fine line between a realistic but aspirational goal and one that will keep you locked in your current condition. I absolutely want you to dream big. Never play small with your dreams, but when it comes to setting goals, be sure the objectives you set can be achieved within your defined timeframe and with the resources you have access to now. The path will widen as you move forward. Keep in mind that while the dream is limitless, the journey requires a plan. A quick example would be the difference between setting a goal to lose 100 pounds in a year versus a more realistic goal to lose 5 pounds a month. You're goals should help you focus on making incremental steps forward. You stick to stretching out your hand. Let God handle dividing the waters.

Time-based – A timeline for your goals is an important part of holding yourself accountable. Timelines are also great encouragement to act. If you're like me, you like to see completion marks on your to-do list. Including a due date for each task will provide you with a sense of accomplishment as you are able to check them off. Many people cannot find the motivation to get tasks done without a written deadline. Even artificial or self-imposed deadlines can provide the kick in the pants to get you into gear.

ACCOUNTABILITY BUDDIES

Establishing accountability will keep you on track towards achieving your goals. This is an excellent opportunity to involve your community of support—your dream team. Share your goals with your family and close friends. Let them know what you plan to achieve and ask them to help you stay focused and on track. This form of accountability can be hugely motivating for many people. Most of us are willing to let ourselves down (we're great at justifying things and making excuses to ourselves), but we have a much more difficult time disappointing loved ones, friends, mentors, and coaches.

The Rooms of Your House:
The Gym

The gym represents the overall state of your health and physical fitness. Another way to think about it is your overall state of activity.

It can include non-gym activities like dancing, outdoor sports, jumping rope, walking, and gardening.

Some other considerations in the gym are any health, stress, and weight management issues.

The key questions you want to ask yourself are:

- Do incorporate movement into my daily routine?
- Do I exercise at least three days every week?

I learned a technique from author and leadership coach Marshal Goldsmith several years ago when I hired him to conduct a workshop for a group of corporate leaders. He encouraged creating an accountability buddy with whom you touch base nearly every day. The buddy asks you three or four specific questions that are tied to your life plan or blueprint. The questions are focused on your dream but your plan. The role of your buddy is not to provide coaching or feedback. It's just a little tickler at the end of the day to remind you to do the things you said you were going to do or point out that you didn't do them. It's a simple accountability system, but it works.

For example, my list includes:

Did you walk for at least 15 minutes today?

Did you drink at least 4 bottles of water today?

Did you meditate/pray this morning?

Did you go to bed by 11pm?

Did you create meaningful content today that you can share with your community?

I have identified these as my "must do's" each day. These are the activities that help me stay on track with living my dream life and focusing on the rooms or areas of my life that I've chosen to prioritize for the next couple of years. My answers to these questions provides me with a quick scan of my progress. Knowing that someone is going to ask me these questions throughout the week keeps me focused.

We all want to make changes to our lives as quickly as possible, but focusing primarily on 3-6 month goals will create a sense of overwhelming urgency, which may make you feel like you have to get it all done tomorrow. That style of short-term thinking will set you up for discouragement and failure because significant transformation takes time.

If you've ever renovated a room in your house, such as the bathroom or kitchen, you know just how much work is involved and how long it takes—and you also know it usually a lot longer than originally anticipated! You're renovating a whole house when it comes to your life, so your dream home isn't going to spring up out of the ground overnight. Give yourself adequate time to accomplish what you set out to change. Keep these guidelines in mind when setting goals:

- 6-12 months = short-term goals

- 12-24 months = medium-term goals

- 2+ years = long-term goals

EXERCISE: SET GOALS

Revisit the Current Living Arrangements Assessment in Chapter 3 and identify three areas that require the most focus in your life. These would be the rooms where you rated yourself a one or a two. In those areas, set two or three goals for each room.

You may be tempted to create more goals, but be careful; too many changes in too many areas of your life all at once can be overwhelming and distracting. Many of us are fooled into thinking busyness is the same as progress, but that is not the case. After 500 times around a race track, a race car hasn't gone anywhere; it ends up close to where it started despite a whole lot of exerted energy. Unlike the race car stuck to the track, your transformation journey is a long one that will cover valleys, mountains, and long open plains, and will thus require stored reserves of energy. Your life's transformation is about focus, patience, and progress over time, not overnight transformations.

Exercise: Set Goals			
Rooms #1:	**Rooms #2:**	**Rooms #3:**	*Instructions: Based on your assessment results, list the 2-3 room that you have chosen to focus on for this activity. Using the SMART framework, write one to three 12-month goals for each room.*
Goal #1:	Goal #1:	Goal #1:	
Goal #2:	Goal #2:	Goal #2:	
Goal #3:	Goal #3:	Goal #3:	
Result:	**Result:**	**Result:**	**Legacy:** *Insert your vision statement here. The results should contribute to this end state.*

10

TAKING ACTION, PART 2 –
DEFEATING PROCRASTINATION

*"What one does is what counts. Not what
one had the intention of doing."*

– PABLO PICASSO

That *thing*. You know what I'm talking about. It's that thing you need to do to achieve your goals. In fact, you don't just need to do it, you want to do it. It's there on your 'to do' list and your goal list, and it contributes to your vision statement. It's been at the front of your mind all day, and you might even be confident that the task will be enjoyable once you get started. There isn't anything more important for you to be working on right now, yet you still aren't doing the thing you know you need to do. You're ignoring it, avoiding it, or endlessly thinking about the best way to come at it. In other words: you're procrastinating.

This must stop.

Getting started is, of course, the hardest part of any project. Implementing change, taking risks, shaking up your life, and accepting the uncomfortable feelings that accompany trying something new is difficult. That's why our natural inclination is to procrastinate.

Living an authentic life should be the most natural thing in the world and perhaps it would be if it weren't for the decades of conditioning and programming we all experience. At the hands of well-meaning parents, family members, bosses, and partners, and society at large, we endure all manner of coaxing just so we can be more of who *they* think we should be. Worse still, who they *need* us to be.

Human beings are creatures of habit. We get comfortable with the routines of 'the way things are.' It's often against our natural instincts to shake things up – even if we aren't happy with the current state of 'the way things are.' While we readily accept the responsibilities and pressures of adulthood, at times we still act like children.

Children don't own homes because they lack the maturity and skills necessary to prioritize care and maintenance. If I were to set my twelve-year-old son loose in a house of his own, he would never make his bed, clean the bathroom, vacuum the floors, or pay the bills. A house would be one big play-zone and he'd assume all the chores would take care of themselves. Chronic procrastination is a way of life for children because keeping up with responsibilities is far less appealing than doing something immediately gratifying.

Work can be an exhilarating experience, especially if we're passionate about achieving our goals, but a lot of the time work feels like... well... work! Procrastination, on the other hand, almost always feels liberating. Avoiding doing something is empowering and even a little rebellious. Chronic procrastinators approach management of their lives in much the same way a 12-year-old would approach taking care of a physical home. They tell themselves their dream life is one that's clutter-free, organized, and stimulating, and yet they consistently make choices that return the opposite results.

To be fair, I'm not exempt from this sneaky behavior, and there are many examples of procrastination in my own life. I rarely procrastinate when it comes to big projects, but the practical day-to-day things seem to always get put off. When you're busy with many projects and activities, it's easy to put the little things off until tomorrow. Then one day you find yourself asking, "Did I write the check and put it in the mail?" "Did I follow-up with that doctor's appointment?" "Did I take my car in to get the oil changed?" "Did I get that tire replaced?" "Did I go grocery shopping?"

Far too often I find myself thinking that I can push the little things out until the end of the week or month. What ends up happening, of course, is the end of the week or month comes and now my To-Do List is twice as long. Procrastination isn't always about avoiding the big scary things, as you might initially assume. It can just as easily be a collection of little day-to-day activities that gather up and then bury you when you least expect it.

PRIORITIZE THE IMPORTANT

In *First Things First*, Stephen Covey et. al.,.argues most people tend to prioritize the urgent matters in our lives. Whatever happens to be demanding our attention at any given moment becomes the fire we need to put out immediately, while more important but less urgent tasks get brushed aside. As a result, we don't give these items the attention they deserve. Unfortunately, this often includes activities such as spending time with family, practicing self-care, and pursuing ongoing education and personal development. These activities are absolutely vital to a full and rich life, but because they aren't demanding our attention *this moment* we let them go until they become emergencies.

Always dealing with the latest crisis is an extremely stressful way to live your life. A valuable lesson from my cancer experience was learning to be comfortable with not getting everything done. For the first time in my life, I finally allowed myself to spend whole days sitting, resting, and healing. I became much more thoughtful about what was urgent and what was important. I couldn't run around juggling a dozen things at once because I needed to save energy for when my son came home from school each day. He understood his mom was battling cancer, but kids need a lot of attention from their parents, regardless of whether their parent is sick or not. I had to conserve my energy, so I could be present mentally, emotionally, and spiritually with my children.

Even if you aren't dealing with a health challenge, you'll still have to manage your energy wisely. There's only so much we can accomplish before we need to rest and recharge. I urge you to get crystal clear on what is truly important to you and direct your energy towards what really needs to be done. When I say need, I mean N-E-E-D. Sometimes we think we've created a list of what 'needs to get done,' but upon closer inspection, it's actually a list of things that 'would be nice to get done.'

EXERCISE: WHY DO I PROCRASTINATE?

There are many reasons we put things off. This exercise will help you determine the reasons you most often procrastinate.

In the chart below, list two to three tasks you've put off for at least three months. Place an **X** in the column indicating your reason for the delay

Exercise: Why Do I Procrastinate?							
Reasons for Procrastination							
Task	Lack of maturity	Lack of skill	Lack of finances	Lack of confidence	Lack of energy	Lack of resources	Other

No one can do this work for you. Even if you've identified specific, measurable, assignable, realistic, and time-bound goals, you still must put effort into achieving them. You must *do* the work. Get up, make changes, and take actions that are different from what you've done up until now.

This is rarely easy.

Human beings prefer not to rock the boat by making changes, even if those changes are going to make their lives better. It's easier to go with the flow and do things as we always have done. Taking action to overcome challenges that have held you back from achieving your goals is going to be some of the most difficult work of your entire life; it'll also be the most rewarding.

EXERCISE: TAKE TWO STEPS

Don't let the fact that you may be behind on your goal freak you out. One way to restart and gather momentum is to think about the next couple of steps or actions you need to take to begin again. For each task you listed in the previous exercise, describe the next **TWO** actions you'll take to move the task toward completion. Then give yourself a deadline to complete each action.

Exercise: Take Two Steps		
Task	Next Two Steps I'll take	Deadline
A.	1. 2.	1. 2.
B.	1. 2.	1. 2.
C.	1. 2.	1. 2.

In one of my *Blueprint* workshops, an attendee made a profound statement. "I'm really great at making plans," he said. "I'm great at spreadsheets. I'm great at creating vision boards. I'm great at making to-do lists. I'm good at all of that. Where I have a problem is in the execution." This was an insightful statement because most people never admit this truth. They trick themselves into believing that the planning and defining the goals is the work, then they're surprised when little changes in their lives.

The only outcome produced from the process of planning is a plan. The real work is taking consistent, often daily action against the plan. Doing the real work means tackling fears head-on. It means expending a great deal of energy to force yourself out of your comfort zone. It means taking risks, possibly falling down and finding the strength to get back up and do it all over again. It's not easy, but you can do it. The secret is to get started immediately.,. Journalist, author and life coach Mel Robbins calls it the **5 Second Rule**.

In my own life, I've discovered that if I can have the discipline to choose targeted action in the first few seconds following any spark of inspiration, I can slowly begin to change old, unproductive patterns. I call those first few seconds my **"5 seconds of power"**. That spark of inspiration, for me, represents universal alignment which is more than half of what any of us need to transform our lives. If you can quickly align with the universe (3-5 seconds), you stand a much greater chance for success than giving your mind a chance to get wind of what's happening and go into "extinguish the spark" mode. So, the next time your alarm clock goes off, or you receive a spark to exercise, make a healthier dietary choice, turn off the TV, call up a friend, hug your kid, or kiss your significant other, act quickly!

11

TAKING ACTION, PART 3 – OVERCOMING FEAR

"It's not the absence of fear, it's overcoming it. Sometimes you've got to blast through and have faith."

– EMMA WATSON

Many of us give up on our dreams because we've learned there's a good chance we're going to run into a brick wall of rejection. Our fear of hearing "no" leads us to not bother to ask the questions we need to ask in the first place. At our core, *fear* controls many of the decisions we make in our lives.

My daughter recently described a nightmare where she was relentlessly chased by a ferocious grizzly bear. No matter how fast she ran, every time she glanced back over her shoulder, the bear was gaining ground.

The bear in the dream likely represented a generalized fear or anxiety in her life, but it nonetheless triggered a visceral response in her brain and body. The ingrained fight or flight response is always accessible, and is governed by the area of our brains known as the amygdala. The amygdala takes over when it perceives danger. This response is triggered regardless of whether the danger is real or imagined.

The Rooms in Your House:
The Home Office

The home office represents your business, career, or job.

The home office is a workspace where you go to strategize, think, and plan. It's also a place to go to carry out the activities identified in your plans. It can also represent time management.

Questions to ask about your home office:

- How satisfied am I with my current career?
- Does my current job support my financial needs?
- If money weren't an issue, would I do my job for free?

When we're trying something new for the first time or making big changes in our lives, we often feel anxious and fearful. These feelings make us want to run away or avoid whatever is causing the uncomfortable emotions. The thinking brain, which is connected to the fear center of the brain, immediately begins searching for patterns so it can decide what to do with this anxiety. But because this is new, it can't find the same situation, so it finds some other memory buried in your unconscious and says "oh, yes. This will due." It then attaches that fear to this new experience. So occasionally we aren't feeling fear but *remembering* fear. There's no real life or death threat, no grizzly bear chasing after us . . . but our bodies don't know that because the brain doesn't do a great job differentiating between reality and memory.

Fear is an emotional response to some stimulus – in most cases a primal and entirely valid response. It lets us know when we're in danger and need to fight or run. In modern life, however, we're rarely in situations where there's actual imminent danger. Much more often we experience a generalized fear in the hippocampus, via projections and memories, that we create ourselves by associating unrelated things or events. Humans are profoundly talented at manufacturing and reinforcing the fears that keep us from moving forward. Luckily, when the source of our own worst fears comes from within, it means it's also within us to find the deep well of courage to overcome them.

You can begin to unlearn manufactured fears by flipping them on their head. (Just be sure you're not trying to take this on during an already stressful time.) The idea is to develop a competing response to the fear instead of succumbing to it. If you can't muster the confidence to develop a competing response on your own, solicit the required reassurance from someone you trust. The goal is to use positive self-talk and affirmations to develop a new narrative to inspire an entirely different emotion other than fear.

If you're afraid of flying, start by telling yourself, "I'm not afraid of flying." If you're afraid of success or failure, tell yourself "I am not afraid of success," or "I'm not afraid of failure." Maybe there's someone you have wanted to approach to ask on a date, but you're afraid of being rejected. Tell yourself, "The world won't end if I or my idea is rejected. I will persist." This approach sounds ridiculously simple, but you'll find it's quite challenging to put into action. The truth in most cases is that if you don't succeed or are rejected, you can handle it. Even in the worst-case scenario it's possible to bounce back so the fear was just a waste of your time.

Another technique to help battle your fear is to come up with a distraction. Our brains are powerful pattern seekers. They like doing and thinking the same thing repeatedly. We now know from the latest research in neuroscience that we can rewire our brains and get rid of old patterns. When an old fear surfaces, think or do something that'll interrupt the pattern. Once you break the old pattern you can instill new habits and better patterns, ones that are more helpful in bringing you towards your goals.

Reflect on your life for a moment. Where have you set goals and objectives that were never accomplished? Maybe you gave up halfway there, or maybe you never even got started. Think about those areas and ask yourself,

"What was I afraid of?" There was something holding you back. If you were able to drum up the motivation to set the goal, yet didn't start, or you stopped before achieving it, there's an invisible barrier of some kind in the way. Until you identify what's holding you back, moving forward is going to be very challenging.

Don't settle for easy answers. Don't cop out and say, "I'm afraid of success" or "I'm scared of failure." We all share those fears. Think about an iceberg. Only a fraction of the iceberg is visible above the surface of the water. Let's call this the "presenting issue". Well if you've watched the movie Titanic, you that the more dangerous part of an iceberg is the much larger, unseen portion underneath the water – the "real issue". Our lives can sometimes be shipwrecked before we even get close to the part of the issue we can see. What limiting beliefs have you internalized? Where did you lose confidence in your ability to outrun the bear or overcome whatever obstacles come your way? Who told you through their words or actions that you're not enough? Reflect on these questions to look below the surface to see what you can discover. It will almost certainly take more than just one sitting to get to the root of your fears. It may take asking yourself these questions over the course of several days, weeks or even months, and listening intently to what comes back.

Over the next few days, look at the areas of procrastination you previously defined, and reflect on the question, "What is my fear really telling me?"

I'm not asking you to stir up fear just for the sake of making yourself more afraid or revisiting old pains. I want you to ask the questions, so you can confront them. It's impossible to address and overcome fears you don't first identify and face. That's why in many mythologies, names are said to hold special powers. In these stories, such as the fairy tale *Rumpelstiltskin* for example, knowing someone's name gives you power over them. It's the same with our fears. Once we identify and name a fear, we're able to tame it.

Fear by Association

Some time fear can strike us and doesn't even originate from our own experiences but can be that of someone else or some tragic event that we experience indirectly.

You might recall the mass shooting tragedy in Colorado in 2012, during which many people were killed in a movie theater at a late-night showing. And more recently in 2017 the mass shooting at the outdoor country music concert in Las Vegas. In both cases, a lone gunman killed dozens of people and injured dozens more. Immediately after the events, people began to associate fear of dying with movie theaters and outdoor concerts. On social media, people posted, "I'm never going to another late-night movie showing," and "This makes me afraid to attend outdoor events." There was a collective fear response and amped up security presence became the norm at subsequent events and venues in the wake of these events.

The best thing many of these people could have done soon after obtaining the proper grief counseling, in my opinion, was to go to a movie theater and enjoy a film or attend an outdoor concert or event. Yes, take the necessary precautions but face it. Allowing fears to fester unchecked only reinforces them. By facing your fears you prevent them from establishing their roots in your brain and body. We should always be cautious especially considering these types of tragedies, but we must resolve never to let them make us so afraid that we stop enjoying our lives.

Exercise: Managing Fear

For this exercise, what I'd like for you to do now is consider a situation that you're afraid to face, and play out a scenario in your head. Imagine that the fear is not there. What would your life be like if you were not afraid? You're rewiring a neural pathway. Keep in mind that I was comfortable in my corporate gig and starting a new business gave me a little anxiety. I had to intentionally imagine what my life would look like if that fear of failure didn't exist. What choice would I make if I remove the fear? Once I removed that as a blocker, the decision was clear, and I took the leap and as it turns out there was nothing to be afraid of.

Most fears are learned. Studies show that humans are born with only two fears: the fear of falling, and fear of loud noises. Everything beyond that is learned. Some of the most common human fears are flying, germs, small spaces, thunder and lightning, dogs, open or crowded spaces, heights, snakes, and spiders. While it may not be fear of spiders, snakes, or heights that has held you back from achieving your dream life, there's a good chance whatever you're afraid of probably has as little likelihood of taking place as you getting bitten by a deadly spider or stumbling across the path of an angry snake.

Exercise: Overcoming Fear

Situation I fear:

_____

_____

_____

_____

What 'competing response' will I use to overcome this fear?

_____

_____

What thought, or activity will I use to distract me when this fear surfaces?

_____

_____

What small steps will I take to move toward the thing I'm afraid of rather than running away?

_____

_____

What can I do to help inspire and reassure myself while I'm unlearning my fears?

_____

_____

After facing the fear head-on, what did I learn?

_____

_____

12

FOCUS: WHERE TO INVEST YOUR TIME AND ENERGY

"Being selective—doing less—is the path of the productive. Focus on the important few and ignore the rest."

– TIMOTHY FERRISS

Most days I feel like I'm battling ADD (Attention Deficit Disorder). I usually have hundreds of thoughts, lists and ideas floating around in my mind. It's a wonder I get anything done. As a matter of fact, this one hundred or so page book that you are holding in your hands right now took me about four years to complete. Why? I lacked the focus and discipline to simply get it done. About 70% of the book was completed within about nine months. I spent the other three years or so in an unfocused but very busy and otherwise productive haze proving that it's possible to be extremely busy while not getting done the main thing you've set out to accomplish.

As you know, the *Blueprint* is an ongoing process. You'll want to revisit the exercises in this book again and again. Your dream house isn't going to appear overnight, so you're going to need to stick with your self-improvement project for the long haul. But how can you possibly stay on track over the course of a journey that may take months, years, or even decades?

The answer is simple: focus.

Consider the difference between lasers and flood lights. They're both light sources, but one of them is a lot more focused than the other. The laser is extremely precise. Thanks to the precision of the laser, doctors and surgeons can cut into a body to access an area while creating a minimal amount of damage. A floodlight, on the other hand, casts a broad glare. You can light up a whole football field with floodlights, but their function is widespread illumination rather than focused intensity. Due to a floodlight's lack of focus, it isn't nearly as specialized a tool as the light from a laser. I spent four years floodlighting through life when what I needed to get the book published was a laser. When it comes to the construction project for designing your dream life, you'll want to be focused like the laser, not broad like the flood light.

"Don't confuse motion and progress. A rocking horse keeps moving but doesn't make any progress."

— ALFRED ARMAND MONTAPERT

Once you've done the (fundamental) foundational work discussed earlier in the book, you'll want to focus your efforts on just two or three rooms at a time. Don't try to tackle the whole house at once. Instead, pick the rooms most in need of attention and focus on improving them within a 12-month horizon. If you take on too much at once, nothing will get done. You end up sending your energy in so many different directions that you don't make any progress.

Balancing Creativity and Focused Attention

Focus can be difficult for smart and creative people because dozens of ideas are flooding their minds in any given moment. In addition, creative people often get asked to share ideas and provide feedback with friends and colleagues. As a result, not only are these people dealing with their own ideas and projects, but usually several other people's projects as well. This makes it harder to sift out the ideas that are meant for their own lives from the ideas meant for others.

Having to focus on one or two things can be a frustrating experience. I have a friend who says it feels like he's killing a part of his soul if he can't have eight plates spinning at once. He can't get a lot accomplished because of his lack of focus, but that's all right with him. It's part of who he is. That's his authentic self.

It all comes back to authenticity. Some people can handle a higher level of chaos and risk-taking regarding what their accomplishments or lack thereof. My friend is perfectly happy taking longer to achieve his goals while enjoying the excitement he feels from having several projects going on at once. That may or may not feel right for you.

Letting the Plates Drop

Constantly dealing with stress, urgencies, and multiple priorities, it hampers creativity. When there are a dozen plates spinning at once and you're responsible for all of them, you aren't planning, and you aren't thinking strategically about your decisions and actions. It's all you can manage just to keep the plates spinning.

It can be difficult to admit we get pleasure from stressing ourselves out, but the truth is many people love drama. They create and then nourish the stress in their lives. You probably know several people who pride themselves on how busy they are. They can't wait to tell you (and anyone else who'll listen) how full their calendars are. They never seem to have down-time and they're always exhausted. I certainly know many people like that. In fact, it used to be me, and I can still turn back into that person if I'm not careful.

Early in my career, I thought success was defined by how many plates I could keep spinning at once. I was wonderful at dealing with chaotic and stressful situations. I would even tell people, "I'm great in a crisis. If something catastrophic happens, you'll want me on your team."

For a person who feels like they need to keep ten plates spinning at all times, the most fearful thing in the world for them is to suddenly stop, let everything drop, and then face the reality that the world did not end.

I realized along the way, however, approaching my career in this manner was impacting my personal life on a lot of different levels. I was inadvertently and subconsciously creating a life that was scattered and chaotic because it was where I felt "on," "alive," and "in the zone." Sitting down bored with nothing to do was a nightmare for me. I couldn't function if there wasn't some sort of craziness going on around me. It took a long time before it finally dawned on me what I was doing to myself. I was always talking about how exhausted and tired I was, and yet I was the one creating the environment that left me feeling drained. Enter a breast cancer diagnosis. The Universe is efficient at presenting us with the necessary tests designed to teach us the lessons we need to learn.

Spinning a dozen plates day in and day out isn't sustainable. You can't live that way forever. At some point, you must prioritize and focus. The choice not to focus is the choice not to make progress. Trying to do it all only facilitates more procrastination and frustration; it's an illusion that you can make real progress without some level of focus.

There's a wonderful quote from Tony Robbins on this topic: "One reason so few of us achieve what we truly want is that we never direct our focus, we never concentrate our power; most people dabble their way through life, never deciding to master anything in particular."

For a person who feels like they need to keep ten plates spinning at all times, the most fearful thing in the world is to all of a sudden stop, let everything drop, and be forced to acknolwedge the world didn't end. Unfortunately, this type of person rarely signs up to stop the craziness and overwhelm voluntarily. Usually, it's life slapping them with a circumstance that forces them to stop and look at life in a different way. Or they experience total burnout. That's when people walk away from marriages and from children. They quit jobs on an emotional whim. They start smoking after having successfully quit. They make terrible decisions because life has become overwhelming. Those feelings could have been avoided if they took time to stop, reflect, and identify the important things that really needed to be focused on.

While your renovation project should focus on a handful of rooms, you're always going to have to multi-task various rooms to some degree. In my own life, The Den (my role as mom), The Safe (my role as entrepreneur), The Bedroom, Gym and the Kitchen (self-care), and The Home Office (personal growth) are areas of focus for me. They are my pillars. They don't get all my attention all the time, but none of them can be totally ignored if I'm going to continue moving forward with designing and living my dream life.

Sometimes when we're in the belly of the beast, surrounded by the demands of work and family, it can be extremely difficult to get the kind of distance we need to reflect accurately on what's most important.

In our dream house metaphor, The Bedroom is our place of relaxation. It's where we go to rest and to recharge our batteries. Unfortunately, most of us rarely give ourselves time and permission to do the necessary re-charging. We're far too busy battling whatever emergency happens to be front of us that day. That's why I'm a big proponent of temporarily getting away from it all to recharge and revise your blueprint.

Two or three times a year I take a vacation by myself. I don't bring my family or friends; it's just me for a night or two away from home. I go to a place where I know I'll be able to recharge – usually that means somewhere near water, like a beach, cottage, or the lake – and I think deeply about my upcoming or ongoing activities, and I analyze the different projects that have found their way into my life. I'm not particular about writing anything down at this point. I just give my mind space and time to wonder, explore, and be creative.

It's time to stop trying to carry the weight of the world on your back. It's time to determine what is important to you and then dedicate much of your time, efforts, money, and resources towards those things.

The responsibilities, obligations, and expectations can become metaphorical bars of a cage that confines our hopes and dreams. If we don't allow the lion out to wander and roar, we'll forget or abandon our goal of embracing the majestic beast that is our true selves. Once I've let the lion out of the cage and given serious thought to everything I'm dealing with, I assess what really belongs on my list of responsibilities.

You would be amazed at how often I discover that much of what consumes my time and energy are other people's issues. And when it comes down to it, fussing over other people's problems doesn't move me towards my goals.

I realized several years ago many of the things stressing me out weren't my responsibilities. I'm the one who agreed to bring them into my life. I signed-up to deal with them. Somebody asked, "Would you mind taking a look at this for me?" and I agreed. Perhaps it was because I didn't want to offend them or it was because I wanted them to think I was a great friend. We all do it: we say *Yes* to things when we know we should say *No*.

When you do this, you'll find yourself spending more and more of your time and energy on other people's problems, activities, challenges, and stresses. We take on their baggage as though it were our own. If helping a close friend or valued colleague is important to you, then by all means take it on. I would simply encourage you to stop long enough to consider whether this altruism is *really* part of your calling. It's not always so. What's more, far too often we say, *yes* before we've even considered the impact it may have on the important things we need to complete.

It's time to stop trying to carry the weight of the world on your shoulders. It's time to determine what's important to you and then dedicate time, effort, money, and resources towards just those things. Approach your dream house project with the focus of a laser, not the vast breadth of a flood light.

EXERCISE: LASER-LIKE FOCUS

This exercise will help you clarify the few critical goals you want to accomplish in the next 9–12 months. Remember what Tony Robbins said: "most people dabble their way through life because they don't decide to master anything." I want you to master the area of your life you deem to be most important. You can do this for other areas of your life as well, but let's use the following exercise to practice focusing on what's most important.

Refer to the Current Living Arrangements assessment in Chapter 3. Which area did you rate as needing the most improvement? For the purposes of this exercise, use that "room". For you to improve one aspect of that area, what goal can you set for yourself to work on over the next 9-12 months? Now break that goal down into 2-4 specific tasks or activities.

Exercise: Getting Focused

Room/Area: _____

Goal Statement: _____

1) What specific activity requires my focused attention?

_____

2) What resources do I have (or can purchase or borrow) to help me focus?

_____

3) What relationships can I leverage? What specifically do I need from each person or group?

_____

4) When will I begin?

_____

5) How will I measure my success and improvement over time?

_____

6) What am I currently doing that should be reprioritized to allow me to focus on this activity/task?

_____

13

The First Law Of Motion

"Whatever the world looks like now. That's not always how it's going to look. There's more. There's always more."

– Patrick Ness, More Than This

Taking action is difficult because we prefer the familiar to the unknown. We find comfort in what we're accustomed to, even when it's something that isn't good for us. Not wanting to disturb the status quo, along with Isaac Newton's First Law of Motion, leads to feeling stuck. If 5th grade was as long ago for you as it is for me, I'll remind you. Essentially, the law states that a body at rest will remain at rest unless acted upon by some external force which is why it is figurately and quite literally difficult to get off the couch and exercise.

This explains why so many people come to me for coaching convinced their lives will never improve, no matter what they do. They say they'll never get the job of their dreams or never have the relationship they want. They're totally convinced they that losing those 50 pounds will remain out of reach. They feel completely trapped. They are caught in a cycle of negativity, and the inertia becomes so frustrating that they sometimes give up and won't even bother trying to get unstuck.

The lack of forward momentum was very real for me even in working to complete this book. Here I am coaching you on overcoming procrastination and getting unstuck and I'm struggling with those same obstacles myself. That's why the "external force" is so critical. I believe in positive self-talk, affirmations and mantras but sometimes you need something or someone outside of yourself to help snap you out of your inertia. For me that turned out to be two annoying but consistent online task reminders. Every morning at 9:30am an alarm would go off on my phone as a reminder to, "FINISH EDITING THE BOOK TRELLIS!" and then again at 9:30pm and I would say to myself, "DJ IS ASLEEP. SPEND AN HOUR EDITING THE BOOK TRELLIS!" I'm not exaggerating when I tell you that 80% of the effort to write this book was spent on the last 20% of editing and re-editing and then editing some more. Talk about perfection getting in the way of progress!

To finally complete this book, I had to behave my way out of inertia. Each day I had to do exactly what I've advised you to do. I had to prioritize and focus. I had to add writing and editing activities to my daily calendar. And when the phone alarmed, and the inspiration struck, I grabbed those 5 seconds of power, took out the laptop and got to work. I can't say that I was perfect but having some external reminder helped me get it across the finish line.

Another very real obstacle to getting unstuck was confronting my fear of rejection. Publishing a book is a very vulnerable endeavor. Scribbling notes in a private journal that no one will ever read is one thing but sharing my insights and very personal experiences publicly is quite another. Our thoughts and experiences are very personal and exposing them to broad criticism and possible rejection from people who don't know and love us takes courage. If I'm honest, that fear was also a cause of my procrastination. I suspect that's why it takes most new authors longer to write and publish their first book compared to subsequent books. So, whether you're writing a book, starting a new business, pursuing a healthier lifestyle, or planning an event, you're never stuck. Find that resource who can serve as your external force and help move you towards your goal.

Knocking Down Walls

Before you build a new house, you need to knock down some or all the walls of the old one. This book is intended to help you topple more than a few walls and let much needed light into the dark corners of your life. My desire for each of you is that you allow the insights you've gained while reading *The Blueprint* open your heart, illuminate your purpose, and help you develop a plan for designing and living a life of authenticity.

Life is dynamic. It includes what we plan for, but also what comes to us as a total surprise. Sometimes all of life's uncertainty can feel like chaos, but I want you to lean into the chaos. Not only can your Blueprint change. It must! No one has all the answers. Just when we think we have the answers to today's challenges, we are hit with some unique scenario that proves we were only repackaging yesterday's ineffective solutions, and we will be even more clueless tomorrow. We're all, to some degree, stumbling our way through life drawing much of the map as we go.

---

*Life is flexible, dynamic, and always growing and changing,
so we need to grow and change right along with it.*

If you've been thoughtful throughout the book and given the exercises the mindfulness, energy, and attention your life deserves, you're on your way! Hopefully you have a few new tactics and techniques that will help you get there in a way that feels right for you.

You Can Always Make a Different Choice

The power of choice is something I remind my coaching clients about nearly every day. You don't like your job? Okay, change it. You're not in love with your house anymore? Move to a new one. If you don't like the window treatments in the living room, don't complain about them; just change them. If you're not satisfied with your physical appearance or your health, make different choices about exercise and nutrition. We might not always be able to choose the consequences of our actions, but we do get to make decisions about where our lives are headed. You're empowered to make different choices than you've made in the past.

The choices we make are like the money we invest in our construction or renovation project. We must make wise choices, as well as make wise *use* of our choices, because when you make a choice, you're usually choosing one thing at the expense of something else. As much as we would all love it, we simply can't go in different directions at once; not if we want to get anywhere. When you choose to be courageous and bold, you're choosing not to give in to fear. You're choosing not to feed the things that'll keep you in the past or hold you down. You're consciously choosing to move forward into the life of your dreams.

Exercise: Your 'I Choose' List

Think back on all of the information we've covered in the book. Recall the epiphanies you've had along the way. Let each one serve as a spark of inspiration and then turn them into actions. From here it's time to define and affirm the choices and commitments you will make to live your best life.

After completing this final exercise, post your list of choices somewhere you'll see them every single day. It could be the bathroom mirror, the sunvisor in your car, the front of the refrigerator, or your laptop screensave. This list will serve as a reminder not only of the choices you've made, but also that you have the power to choose daily.

This is your life, and yours alone. You are empowered and responsible to make it the absolute best it can be. My goal isn't to prescribe what your life should look or feel like. If it's working for you, feels authentic, and is moving towards your broader purpose, I say do it and keep on doing it. The moment your approach stops bringing you closer to your divine, universal calling, you can always return to the Bathroom of the Blueprint, look in that mirror, and take a long and honest look at what might be holding you back or getting you off track.

Sometimes we tell ourselves things are making us happy, but there's a faint voice deep inside whispering, *"that is not true"*. The voice tells us what we're doing or how we're doing it isn't bringing us happiness, yet we ignore it because it's easier to continue doing life as we always have rather than change.

It takes courage and tenacity to look at your life and admit you've been giving yourself a pass and what you're doing isn't getting you the life you deserve. Realize that you have the power within you to make different choices and the universe itself is working all things together for your good! Embrace that power as you complete the I Choose List.

Exercise - Your "I Choose" List

List five choices that you are committed to make to improve your life and bring you closer to living the life of your dreams.

1. I choose to…

_____

_____

2. I choose to…

_____

_____

3. I choose to…

_____

_____

4. I choose to…

_____

_____

5. I choose to…

_____

_____

14

YOU'RE JUST BEGINNING

"Never underestimate the power of dreams and the influence
of the human spirit. We are all the same in this notion:
The potential for greatness lives within each of us."

— WILMA RUDOLPH

We are nearing the end of our journey together, but your own personal transformation journey has only just begun.

When renovating a house, you can often improve its value. It's not unheard of for a homeowner to spend $10K renovating a kitchen and thereby increasing the value of the house by two or three times that amount. These are the kinds of exponential returns you will experience when you continue to make major renovations to your life.

However, the value of a home is only partially determined by the house itself. The homes' location will also have an enormous impact on its' overall value along with the condition of the other homes around it.

If your house is part of community where people mow their lawns and quickly repair damage to their homes, the value of your home will benefit from that environment. Similarly, if you live in a community with overgrown lawns, yards full of garbage, and run-down houses, the value of your home will depreciate, regardless of how well you keep it maintained. This is because community matters immensely.

The process outlined in this book is mainly an individual endeavor. You've been focused on determining how best to put more intention into making the changes that will move you closer to the life of your dreams. But you're not doing any of this work in a vacuum. Even though our personal journeys are unique depending on who we are, no man or woman is an island.

A few weeks before the final edits to this book, I spent a long weekend in the north Georgia mountains with three of my closest sister-friends. As is typical with our girl's trips, we spent some of our time together expressing our appreciation and gratitude for our circle and each other. I'm always humbled and extremely grateful that these women love me and appreciate having me in their lives as I do having them in mine. The truth is that I don't exist as the person I am today without the years of love, support, and refining that these friendships have given me. As a person whose purpose is to assist others in finding theirs, these women have been my refuge. Within this small circle of women, I am free to be my authentic self. The me that is intuitive, faithful, positive, compassionate, empathic and generous. But also, the me that uses a lot of profanity, is occasionally politically incorrect, afraid, selfish, withdrawn and angry.

I've grown into becoming not by theoretical, intellectual conversation but by living and experimenting. I know more about authentic self because I've expanded and contracted my boundaries and beliefs and tested absolutes many of which turned out to be only assumptions. Figuring out who you really are is messy and not everyone can witness your messy years and love rather than judge and punish you for them. We're all part of larger networks, families, organizations, and communities. We're connected to one another as human beings. We're drawn to others because community gives us strength.

We're here on this planet Earth to serve one another. You'll find joy in improving your life, but you'll find *fulfillment* by doing it within the context of a community. In the same way the surrounding neighborhood can appreciate or depreciate the value of a home, the people we surround ourselves with will have a significant influence on the quality of our lives. As Jim Rohn famously posited, "You are the average of the five people you spend the most time with." Now I don't know if five is the exact number, but what I do know is if you spend a significant portion of your time surrounded by people who consistently strive to get better, live a life of purpose, uncover their passions, and achieve their goals, it can't help but rub off on you. By the same token, if you hang around with people who aren't striving to be the best and highest possible version of themselves – if they're comfortable maintaining the status quo and holding on to limiting beliefs – it's going to impact you as well.

Now that advice doesn't mean you should absolutely avoid anyone who isn't striving to improve. Far too often we approach life from the standpoint of, "What can I gain from those around me?" We surround ourselves with excellent people because we want them to have a positive impact on us, which is, of course, fantastic but it's also important that you embrace opportunities to **BE** the positive impact on others.

I openly admit that where I live is quite nice. There are beautiful houses, good schools, parks, trails, and plenty of access to shopping and recreation, not to mention some great restaurants. But what I really enjoy about where I live are my great neighbors.

I wasn't the most neighborly person when we first moved in several years ago. We kept to ourselves and did that "friendly wave" thing when we saw neighbors pulling out of their driveways or running to grab a letter from the mailbox, but that was about it. Something shifted when I was nearing the end of my fight with breast cancer and I remembered the importance of community. I became much more intentional about helping build the type of community I wanted to be a part of, a community of positivity, compassion, and support. What's the point of beating cancer and living the life of your dreams if everyone around you is still living unfulfilling lives? I also owe much of this to my son who is the unofficial Mayor of our street. He considers it his duty to introduce himself to every person on our street. He lives the ideal of community. It's in his bones. When he was much younger this concerned me because he really didn't understand the concept of "stranger danger". His approach to dealing with a stranger was to introduce yourself and turn them into a friend.

Never underestimate the impact you can have in this world! You may not yet be living your dream life, and you may have many challenges ahead of you, but trying to improve yourself and the state of the world around you will inspire others to improve their lives.

Ask yourself: *How can I express generosity? How can I impart intention and purpose so that people will benefit from encountering me?*

As you've learned, *The Blueprint* is a dynamic, ongoing process, not an end state. A dream house is never fully completed because the dreamer and the dream are always evolving.

Things will happen along the way that'll require you to adjust and try doing things differently. You may reach your desired dream life five years from now, but when you retire and your kids grow-up and move away, it'll be time to downsize and your plan may change again. You'll be right back to renovating your life e.

I heard Oprah Winfrey say something a few years ago when she was doing a home makeover surprise for one of her viewers, "Your home should rise up to meet you." My hope is that not only will your home rise to meet you, but that your life will also rise to meet you.

This book has been about how you can change your life for the better, but in changing ourselves we change the world around us. That's the real secret behind all of what we have discussed in *The Blueprint*. Not only do you have the power within you to improve your life, you have the power to change the world.

The End

ABOUT THE AUTHOR

Trellis USHER spent nearly twenty years in corporate America and has an extensive background in human capital management, leader and organization effectiveness. After leaving her corporate career behind, Trellis founded her own management consulting firm, T.R. Ellis Group, in 2011 and still works with some of the world's largest brands to develop innovative and inclusive people strategies and solutions.

As an author, entrepreneur, and coach, Trellis devotes her energy to helping individuals and organizations live and operate with more intention and authenticity. As a breast cancer survivor, Trellis advocates and promotes awareness on behalf of other survivors and patients. Other humanitarian causes include increasing the number of women executives and business owners, eradicating homelessness and fostering dialogue to create inclusive cultures so that every person can reach their highest potential.

Trellis has two children and resides in Atlanta, GA.

ACKNOWLEDGMENTS

To all my family members, friends and colleagues, thanks for believing in me. To my breast cancer survivor community, thanks for your courage and inspiration. To Ford Motor Company, Models of Courage/Warriors in Pink, thank you for providing me with a platform to advocate for patients and survivors. To Dr. Kelly May, Dr. Elizabeth Steinhaus and a host of physicians, technicians and nurses, thanks for helping to keep me around a little longer.

Angene, Sophie, Honorene and Robert, thanks for your constant love and support and for being the first ones to encourage me to write this book. Thanks for creating safe spaces for me to learn, succeed, fail, experiment, and grow. Your friendship means more to me than you know.

Bernard aka Doc aka Turk, my favorite, little, big brother. Whenever I think about all that you mean to me, I cry. Dad, thanks for stepping in when it matters most. You are still the funniest person I know. I love you both so much.

Brittany and DJ, being your mom is one of the great joys of my life. I'm in awe of your compassion, kindness and empathy. I'm grateful for your love, support and grace when I'm exhausted and distracted. I'm excited to watch you continue growing into all that you are.

Works Cited

Covey, Stephen et. al., *First Things First.* Mango Media Inc, 2016.

Donne, John. *Devotions upon Emergent Occasions, and Severall Steps in My Sickeness,* 1624.

Doran, G. T. "There's a S.M.A.R.T. way to write management's goals and objectives," *Management Review,* 1981.

Hughes, Langston. "Harlem," *The Collected Poems of Langston Hughes.* Vintage Classics, 1995.

Kondo, Marie. *The Life-Changing Magic of Tidying Up.* Ten Speed Press, 2015.

LeDoux, Joseph. *The Emotional Brain: The Mysterious Underpinnings of Emotional Life.* Simon & Schuster, 1998.

Lowitt, Bruce. "Bannister stuns world with 4-minute mile." St. Petersburg Time, 1999.

Maslow, Abraham. "A Theory of Human Motivation," *Psychological Review,* 1943.

Pillary, Srini, M.D. The Unfocused Mind.

Robbins, Mel. *The 5 Second Rule: Transform Your Life, Work and Confidence with Everyday Courage.* Savio Republic, 2017.